Jürgen Meyer

FOCUS ON MISTAKES

Grammatik und Übungen
für die Sekundarstufe II

Cornelsen
& OXFORD

Focus on Mistakes

Grammatik und Übungen für die Sekundarstufe II

Verfasser Jürgen Meyer, Fachberater für Englisch, Schleswig-Holstein

Verlagsredaktion Christine House unter Mitarbeit von Jewell Hill-Loock, München und Fritz Preuß, Berlin

Buchgestaltung und Herstellung Dirk Risch, Berlin

1. Auflage

5.	4.	3.	2.	
1997	96	95	94	93

Die letzten Ziffern bezeichnen Zahl und Jahr des Druckes.

Alle Drucke dieser Auflage können, weil untereinander unverändert, im Unterricht nebeneinander verwendet werden.

Bestellnummer 37 789

Satz DSD · Demmer Satz+Daten GmbH, Berlin
Druck Fürst&Sohn, Berlin

ISBN 3-8109-3778-9

Vertrieb Cornelsen Verlag, Berlin

Vorwort

Focus on Mistakes richtet sich an Schülerinnen und Schüler der Sekundarstufe II. Es dient der Wiederholung und Festigung von Stoffgebieten aus der englischen Grammatik und beruht auf der Erkenntnis, daß bestimmte Strukturen und sprachliche Erscheinungen dem Lernenden erfahrungsgemäß immer wieder Schwierigkeiten machen und zu Fehlern führen.

Focus on Mistakes versteht sich nicht als systematische Grammatik, sondern vielmehr als Übungsbuch, das sowohl lehrbuchbegleitend als auch -unabhängig einsetzbar ist. Es dient der Überprüfung der Grammatikkenntnisse und soll helfen, Unsicherheiten zu beseitigen. Dabei konnten, wie angedeutet, naturgemäß nicht sämtliche grammatische Themen behandelt werden, sondern schwerpunktmäßig nur solche, die besondere Schwierigkeiten bereiten.

Die einzelnen Kapitel sind so aufgebaut, daß in einem kognitiven Teil zunächst Informationen in Form von Mustersätzen gegeben werden. Die in deutsch abgefaßte Regel dient dazu, den jeweiligen Sachverhalt eindeutig zu klären. Es folgen die entsprechenden Übungen, die sowohl in der Klasse als auch im häuslichen Selbststudium oder im Rahmen von Nachhilfestunden zur Festigung durchgearbeitet werden können. Da die Übungen keinerlei Progression aufweisen, steht die Reihenfolge der Behandlung im Belieben des Lernenden und sollte sich nach seinen persönlichen Erfordernissen richten.

Die phonetische Umschrift folgt der 14. Auflage des **Everyman's English Pronouncing Dictionary** von D. Jones und A.C. Gimson (London 1988).

In den Übungsabschnitten zum **Wortschatz** wird auf Erklärungen weitestgehend verzichtet, da er im allgemeinen als bekannt vorausgesetzt werden kann.

Um den Übungseffekt zu erhöhen, ist es ratsam, sämtliche Übungen stets schriftlich auszuführen und dabei ganze Sätze zu verwenden. Dieses Prinzip sollte besonders in den Kapiteln über das **Verb (5)**, die **indirekte Rede (6)** und die **Bedingungssätze (7)** befolgt werden, um das sprachliche Gefühl intensiver zu schulen. Zu diesem Zweck wird dringend empfohlen, ein Übungsheft anzulegen, damit ein Ausfüllen der Lücken im Buch vermieden wird und der Aufgabenapparat somit mehrfach durchgearbeitet werden kann. Der Lösungsschlüssel ermöglicht jederzeit eine Kontrolle.

Herausgeber und Verlag wünschen beim Studium von **Focus on Mistakes** viel Erfolg.

Inhalt

1

Der Artikel

A Der bestimmte Artikel

Der bestimmte Artikel **the** ist aus dem Pronomen this/that entstanden und hat dadurch noch eine starke demonstrative Bedeutung. Der (Nicht-)Gebrauch des bestimmten Artikels ist in vielen Fällen sehr fehlerträchtig.

Ohne Artikel

Der bestimmte Artikel steht nicht bei Allgemeinbegriffen, aus denen kein Einzelwesen oder -ding besonders hervorgehoben werden soll.

Children like chocolate.

Singular

Eigennamen, auch in Verbindung mit einem Attribut

John was looking at the book. Mary left Europe for America. Uncle Bob, Queen Mary, Fleet Street, Mt. Everest, East Sussex, French Literature, Little John

Zeitbestimmungen

I prefer spring to autumn.

Abstrakta

Time is money. School is over. He went to prison.

religiöse Begriffe

Heaven and Hell

Stoffnamen

Gold is more precious than silver.

Plural

Gattungsnamen

Cats and dogs are people's favourite pets. I like apples and oranges.

Es gibt einige feststehende Ausdrücke, die – anders als im Deutschen – ohne Artikel gebraucht werden.

to be in office	*im Amt sein*
to be in power	*an der Macht sein*
to keep in mind	*im Gedächtnis bewahren*
to go by bus, train, etc.	*mit dem Bus, der Bahn fahren*
to go by air, sea	*auf dem Luft-, Seeweg reisen*
to lose sight of something	*aus den Augen verlieren*
at first sight	*auf den ersten Blick*
in practice	*in der Praxis*
in case	*im Falle*

Mit Artikel

Der bestimmte Artikel wird dann verwendet, wenn in Gedanken/Worten ein Einzelwesen oder -ding aus einer Menge gleichartiger besonders betont werden soll.	The children in our street like chocolate.
Eigennamen, Stoffnamen und Abstrakta + **of** oder Relativsatz	At the time of the Flood.
Abstrakta	The gold that he found was pure.
geographische Namen und Familiennamen im Plural	We always spend our holidays in the Highlands. The Johnsons are our neighbours.
Namen von Flüssen und Meeren	The Thames flows into the English Channel.
Himmelsrichtungen	California is in the west. He lives in the east. *Aber:* from north to south
Tageszeiten in Verbindung mit **in** und **during**	in the morning, during the night
Gattungsnamen als Eigennamen	the Tower, the City
Himmelskörper	the sun, the moon
Es gibt einige Ausdrücke, die – anders als im Deutschen – mit dem bestimmten Artikel verwendet werden.	it is the custom — *es ist üblich* with the exception of — *mit Ausnahme von* at the expense of — *auf Kosten* with the help of — *mit Hilfe von* in the presence of — *in Gegenwart von*

Übung 1

Setze den bestimmten Artikel, wo erforderlich.

Imagine you are □[1] Alice, stepping through □[2] looking-glass, and suddenly everything is reversed. □[3] doorknobs are on □[4] wrong side of □[5] doors. □[6] gear-lever in your car is in □[7] wrong place. □[8] handles on □[9] tin-openers are on □[10] wrong side and turn □[11] wrong way.

□[12] millions of □[13] people wake up every day in just such a predicament. They are left-handed and must face □[14] built-in bias of a world designed for □[15] right-handed majority. In a society of □[16] rights and righteousness, □[17] leftie is left with □[18] leftovers and left-handed compliments. Why we are left- or right-handed remains one of □[19] great unsolved mysteries of □[20] science. We know that nearly two out of every three lefties are male and that left-handedness runs in □[21] families. According to one study, almost half □[22] offspring of □[23] two left-handed parents will take after them.

On □[24] other hand, heredity alone cannot explain □[25] lefties. At least 84 per cent of them are born of □[26] two right-handed parents. And in 12 per cent of □[27] genetically identical twins, one will be right-handed, □[28] other left. *Reader's Digest, Dec. 1988*

Übung 2

Setze den bestimmten Artikel, wo erforderlich.

1 He was an expert on □ English literature.
2 □ industry is a very important branch of □ modern economy.
3 Last summer they travelled down □ Rhine.
4 □ East Anglia has one of □ nicest landscapes in Great Britain.
5 They came over from □ Spain.
6 □ hospital was opposite □ post office.
7 □ cats are very popular pets.
8 □ President of the United States is elected for four years.
9 He took a lively interest in □ modern history.
10 British people like to drink □ tea on almost all occasions.
11 □ history of this country is unfortunately marked by many wars.
12 In many parts of □ Europe □ summer of 1989 was very hot.
13 He crossed □ USA from □ west to □ east.
14 They travelled by □ boat to Great Britain.
15 During □ cold winter many people died.
16 She was born in □ January.
17 □ Monday is □ first day of □ week.
18 Stratford lies on □ Avon.

Übung 3

Setze den bestimmten Artikel, wo erforderlich.

1 When does □ service begin?
2 Where has □ life come from?
3 □ Empire State Building is one of □ highest buildings in □ world.
4 □ south of France is a very popular area for holidays.

5 We should always help □ old and □ poor.
6 □ storks are almost extinct.
7 He paid him by □ hour.
8 He can play □ piano.
9 We didn't have □ patience to listen to him.
10 □ history of this church is very interesting.
11 □ bread is made from □ wheat.
12 There are many aircraft in □ sky.
13 □ Alps offer a very scenic view.
14 A lot of □ people emigrated from □ West Indies to Great Britain.
15 □ policeman told him that □ bank was just round the corner.

B Der unbestimmte Artikel

Der unbestimmte Artikel **a**/**an** ist aus dem Pronomen **one** entstanden und bezeichnet ein Einzelwesen oder -ding.

Mit Artikel

Wie im Deutschen steht der unbestimmte Artikel bei folgenden Ausdrücken:

at a blow	*auf einen Schlag*
at a glance	*auf einen Blick*
in a word	*mit einem Wort*
in a day	*an einem Tag*

Anders als im Deutschen bezeichnet der unbestimmte Artikel die Zugehörigkeit eines einzelnen zu einer Gruppe.

Beruf	He is a teacher.
Religion	He was a Calvinist.
nach **as**	I gave it to him as a present.

Der unbestimmte Artikel steht auch bei
Zeiteinheiten
Mengen- und Maßeinheiten

She travelled 1000 miles a week.
This is only 15p a pound.
The beer was 95p a pint.

Der unbestimmte Artikel wird bei folgenden Wörtern nachgestellt:

many	He has written many a book.
half	It weighs half a pound.
quite	Thursday was quite a nice day.

rather	The play was rather a failure. *Aber:* It was a rather interesting book.	
such	It is such a nice day!	
what (zählbar)	What a lovely day! *Aber:* What nonsense! (nicht zählbar)	

Anders als im Deutschen steht der unbestimmte Artikel bei folgenden Ausdrücken:

to be in a hurry	*in Eile sein*
to have a temperature	*Fieber haben*
to have a cough	*Husten haben*
to have a headache	*Kopfschmerzen haben*
it's a pity	*es ist schade*
in a loud voice	*mit lauter Stimme*
as a rule	*in der Regel*
in a high degree	*in besonderem Maße*
for a change	*zur Abwechslung*
in a friendly manner	*auf freundliche Art*
as a whole	*als Ganzes*
without a break	*ohne Unterbrechung*
to make a noise	*Lärm machen*

Ohne Artikel

nach **to turn** (werden)	He turned communist.
to become	She became president of the club.

Übung 1

Setze den unbestimmten Artikel, wo erforderlich.

1 He decided to be ☐ teacher.
2 Mr Smith is ☐ Scotsman.
3 Harold Wilson was ☐ Prime Minister for many years.
4 Don't make such ☐ noise.
5 He shouted at him in ☐ loud voice.
6 This is quite ☐ nice house.
7 The front window looked out on ☐ busy road.
8 What ☐ silly thing to say.
9 As ☐ boy of five he was able to read fluently.
10 We can go by ☐ car if you want to.
11 One of the robbers turned ☐ informer and told the police about the crime.
12 We had ☐ plenty of time to visit him.
13 I've never seen such ☐ nice house.
14 He was elected ☐ captain of the team.

Übung 2

Übersetze und benutze **half, such, what, many, quite, rather.**

1 Eine halbe Stunde später fuhr sie ab.
2 Was für Unsinn redest du da!
3 Er traf ziemlich viele Leute auf seiner Reise.
4 Er war ein recht guter Fußballspieler.
5 Ich habe noch nie einen so schweren Sturm erlebt.
6 Es war ein ziemlich kalter Tag.
7 Manch ein erfolgreicher Geschäftsmann endet in Armut.
8 Er ist ein ziemlich guter Tennisspieler.
9 Er hat in seiner Jugend manchen Berg bestiegen.
10 Sie hatte noch nie einen so herrlichen Sonnenuntergang gesehen.

Übung 3

Setze den unbestimmten Artikel, wo erforderlich.

1 As ☐ student he often had to work late at night.
2 What ☐ lovely weather.
3 After work he had ☐ good appetite.
4 As ☐ rule, the climate there is rather mild.
5 Can you help me for ☐ change?
6 The house is in ☐ dreadful condition.
7 As ☐ Englishman he always likes a good cup of tea.
8 To ☐ great extent, he was responsible for the crime.
9 He was in ☐ hurry to catch the train.
10 What ☐ kind of ☐ music do you like best?
11 ☐ milk used to be 20p ☐ pint.
12 He made ☐ terrible noise when he entered the room.
13 He studied hard to be ☐ doctor.
14 It was a great exception that Roosevelt was elected ☐ President of the United States three times.
15 I wish you ☐ Merry Christmas and ☐ Happy New Year.

2

Das Adjektiv

Das Adjektiv kennzeichnet die Eigenschaft einer mit einem Substantiv bezeichneten Person/Sache.

Die Steigerungsformen des Adjektivs

1 Die Steigerung mit Hilfe von **-er** und **-est** bei	
– einsilbigen Adjektiven	great, greater, greatest
– zweisilbigen Adjektiven auf **-y**	easy, easier, easiest
– zweisilbigen Adjektiven auf **-le**	able, abler, ablest
– zweisilbigen Adjektiven auf **-ow**	narrow, narrower, narrowest
2 Die Steigerung mit Hilfe von **more** und **most** bei	
– drei- und mehrsilbigen Adjektiven	difficult, more/most difficult
– zweisilbigen Adjektiven, die auf der ersten Silbe betont werden	cautious, more/most cautious
– aus Partizipien entstandenen Adjektiven	interesting, more/most interesting
– abgeleiteten Adjektiven auf **-ly**	friendly, more/most friendly

3 Die unregelmäßige Steigerung

good	better	best	
bad	worse	worst	
much/many	more	most	
little	less	least	
near	nearer	nearest	*(räumlich)*
		next	*(Reihenfolge)*
old	older	oldest	
	elder	eldest	*(bei Familienmitgliedern)*
far	further	furthest	*(bildlich)*
	farther	farthest	*(räumlich)*
late	later	latest	*(zeitliches Verhältnis)*
	latter	last	*(Reihenfolge)*

4 Gebrauch der Steigerungsformen im Vergleich

as . . . as	He is as tall as his brother.
taller/more cautious than	He is taller/more cautious than his brother.
not as (so) . . . as	He is not as (so) tall as his brother.
less . . . than	He is less cautious than his brother.

Substantivierung des Adjektivs

the + Adjektiv, wenn die Gesamtheit gemeint ist

the blind *(die Blinden)* — the blind man *(der Blinde)*

the + Nationalitätenbezeichnung auf **-sh** und **-(t)ch**

the English — the English girl
the French — the French woman
the Dutch — the Dutch government

Das Stützwort one/ones

Um die Wiederholung eines zählbaren Substantivs zu vermeiden, kann man das Stützwort **one/ones** einsetzen.

This book is much nicer than the other one.

One/ones darf nicht nach **own** und Zahlwörtern eingesetzt werden.

Would you like to borrow my car?
No, thanks. I'll use my own.

"Next time you decide to fight a boy, choose one who's smaller than you and whose father's smaller than me!"

Übung 1

Bilde den Komparativ und Superlativ der folgenden Adjektive.

1 comfortable
2 noisy
3 noble
4 lovely
5 hot
6 bad
7 exciting
8 young
9 remote
10 polite
11 beautiful
12 appropriate
13 good
14 muddy
15 lovable
16 low
17 clear
18 loving
19 interested
20 patient
21 large
22 decent
23 small
24 clever
25 tall
26 splendid
27 quiet
28 dull
29 poor
30 delicate
31 dis-appointed
32 stern
33 significant
34 certain
35 mean
36 simple

Übung 2

Setze ein: **more . . . than, not as . . . as, less . . . than, as . . . as.**

1 My boy-friend is □ old □ my brother, but older □ my sister. *(nicht so – wie, als)*
2 For me, chemistry is □ interesting □ physics. *(mehr – als)*
3 England is □ big □ France. *(nicht so – wie)*
4 My friend is □ good at maths □ I am. *(nicht so – wie)*
5 This car is □ expensive □ that one. *(nicht so – wie)*
6 Food costs □ in England □ in Germany. *(weniger – als)*
7 John is □ strong □ his father. *(nicht so – wie)*
8 I get □ pocket money □ my brother, but my sister gets □ him. *(weniger – als, mehr – als)*
9 Our new house is □ big □ our old one. *(nicht so – wie)*
10 Our last holiday was □ exciting □ this one. *(mehr – als)*

Übung 3

Setze die richtigen Steigerungsformen ein.

1 Can you tell me the way to the □ post office? (near)
2 He stormed out of the house without any □ remarks. (far)
3 This is my □ book, I hope it won't be my □ . (late)
4 The policeman told me to take the □ turning to the right. (near)
5 I can't give you □ information on this subject. (far)
6 I haven't been □ north than Manchester. (far)
7 Who will be the □ Prime Minister of Great Britain? (near)
8 Look at that horrible dress. It's the □ fashion. (late)
9 Which films do you prefer – serious or funny ones? I prefer the □ . (late)
10 There was a stop sign, so I couldn't drive any □ . (far)
11 Have you heard the □ news? (late)
12 Whose turn is it □? (near)
13 They left the □ evening. (near)
14 Here are two books: one on history and one on literature. Would you like the first one or would you prefer the □? (late)

Übung 4

Das substantivierte Adjektiv. Übersetze!

1 *(Das Schlimmste)* of the exam is over.
2 Norman Mailer wrote the novel *(Die Nackten und die Toten)*.
3 *(Die Verwundeten)* could not be treated.
4 *(Das Bessere)* is the enemy of *(des Guten)*.
5 *(Der Tote)* could not be identified.
6 *(Die Erfahrenen)* knew what lay ahead of them.
7 He felt sorry for *(die Armen)*.
8 *(Die Holländer)* are a seafaring nation.
9 *(Das Schlimmste)* was that he was completely helpless.
10 *(Der Blinde)* could not find his way.
11 *(Die Kranken)* could not be taken to hospital in time.
12 *(Das Unbekannte)* was always frightening for her.
13 *(Die Blinden)* were supported by the government.
14 *(Das Folgende)* was familiar to him.
15 *(Die Angeklagte)* could not answer any more.

Übung 5

Setze **one/ones** ein, wo erforderlich.

1 He was not the only ☐ in the family to become famous.
2 It is a fact that the rich ☐ play an important role in our society.
3 His left arm was shorter than his right ☐.
4 The first guests arrived for breakfast and the last ☐ left long after midnight.
5 Which is the fastest car – the black ☐, the white ☐, or the red ☐ ?
6 My grandmother is very fond of grapes. She likes green ☐ and black ☐.
7 My mother has bought me a new pen. Unfortunately, it is the wrong ☐.
8 Have you seen my pencil case? – Which ☐ do you mean?
9 He bought her a new skirt because she didn't like her old ☐.
10 Every weekend my mother bakes three cakes, one for me and the other two ☐ for my sister.
11 This winter was colder than the last ☐.
12 Let's look after our planet – it's the only ☐ we have.
13 Don't forget to bring me some books from the library. – Which ☐ do you want?
14 Would you like to borrow my dictionary? – No, thanks, I've got my own ☐.

Übung 6

Komparativ oder Superlativ?

1 This is ☐ thing that could happen to me. (unpleasant)
2 ☐ now than never. (good)
3 On that cruise she was ☐ than ever before. (sick)
4 In the second exam he was ☐ than in the first one. (successful)
5 He didn't care in ☐. (little)

6 She is about ☐ woman I have ever met. (vain)
7 This time he made ☐ mistakes than in his last paper. (few)
8 That was ☐ I could do for you. (little)
9 Today we cannot go for a walk because it is ☐ than yesterday. (wet)
10 Last year our hotel was ☐ than this year. (noisy)
11 Nowadays people smoke ☐ cigarettes than they used to. (few)
12 Twenty is ☐ than twenty-one. (little)
13 Please behave yourself and make a bit ☐ noise. (little)
14 This was ☐ experience in his life. (exciting)
15 There were certainly ☐ places than this village. (pleasant)
16 The second entrance was even ☐ than the first one. (narrow)
17 She is considered one of ☐ dramatists of our time. (great)
18 This is ☐ idea you could have had. (silly)
19 He was ☐ than all the other boy-friends she had had. (handsome)
20 He seemed to have become ☐ every time I saw him. (thin)
21 The perfume smelt ☐ than she had expected. (nice)
22 The ☐ we finish this project, the ☐ . (soon, good)
23 I've never seen a ☐ woman than her. (elegant)
24 He was ☐ man in town. (rich)

"Is it cheaper to fill up with litres or gallons?"

3

Das Adverb

Ein Adverb kann ein Verb, ein Adjektiv oder ein anderes Adverb näher bestimmen:

Verb	He speaks English fluently.
Adjektiv	It is a very nice picture.
Adverb	She sings extremely well.

Adverbarten

Adverbien des Grades stehen gewöhnlich vor dem Verb.

hardly, only, nearly
He particularly enjoyed the concert.

Adverbien der Art und Weise stehen meist am Ende.

slowly, quickly
She shouted at him angrily.

Adverbien der unbestimmten Häufigkeit stehen meist vor dem Verb.

rarely, usually
She usually reads before she goes to bed.

Adverbien der bestimmten Häufigkeit stehen meist am Ende.

They meet monthly.

Adverbien des Ortes stehen meist am Ende.

here, below, far, inside
I'll wait inside. The people are here.

Adverbien der Zeit stehen meist am Anfang oder am Ende.

early, afterwards, lately
We arrived early. Afterwards, we ate.
Aber: We have just eaten.

Adverbien, die einen Satz modifizieren, stehen meist am Anfang.

suddenly, luckily
Suddenly, the door opened.

Bildung der Adverbien

Die meisten Adverbien werden von Adjektiven oder Partizipien durch Anfügen von **-ly** gebildet.

quick → quickly	moving → movingly	excited → excitedly
Aber: due → duly	simple → simply	systematic → systematically
easy → easily	full → fully	friendly → in a friendly manner

Die Steigerung der Adverbien

mit **more/most** zwei- und mehrsilbige Adverbien	clearly interestingly	more/most clearly more/most interestingly
mit **-er/-est** Adverbien ohne Endung (ursprüngliche Adverbien)	soon, sooner, soonest	
Adverbien, die mit dem Adjektiv identisch sind	fast, faster, fastest	
Die unregelmäßige Steigerung	well, better, best a little, less, least badly, worse, worst much, more, most far, farther, farthest *(räumlich)* far, further, furthest *(bildlich)*	

Form und Bedeutung der Adverbien

Einige Adverbien und Adjektive mit gleicher Form und gleicher Bedeutung	daily, monthly, yearly, weekly	I like the daily news. We see him daily.
	enough, fast, hard, long, low	She is a fast driver. You speak too fast.
	better, last, less, least	He is the better one. She sings better than him.

Adverbien mit verschiedenen Formen und unterschiedlicher Bedeutung	close	*dicht*	He sat close beside me.
	closely	*genau*	I watched him closely.
	hard	*schwer*	He works hard.
	hardly	*kaum*	He hardly works.
	fair	*ehrlich*	He played fair.
	fairly	*ziemlich*	He played fairly well.
	late	*spät*	We arrived late.
	lately	*kürzlich*	I've been working hard lately.
	near	*nahe*	He lives quite near the church.
	nearly	*beinahe*	He nearly collapsed.
	short	*kurz*	The driver stopped short.
	shortly	*in Kürze*	He will be back shortly.
Adverbien und Adjektive mit gleicher Form, aber unterschiedlicher Bedeutung	ill	*krank*	to be taken ill
		schlecht	to be ill-treated
	still	*still*	still waters
		noch	Are you still there?
	only	*einzig*	the only son
		nur, erst	only four

very	*genau*	that very day
	sehr	very good
pretty	*hübsch*	a pretty girl
	ziemlich	pretty tired

Nach einigen Verben, die einen Zustand oder eine Eigenschaft ausdrücken, stehen Adjektive, nicht Adverbien. Adjektive stehen auch nach Verben, die die Veränderung eines Zustands ausdrücken.

to become	The sky became clear.
to feel	She felt unhappy.
to get	He got really angry.
to grow	He grew pale.
to look	She looked sad.
to remain	He remained silent.
to seem	He seemed nervous.
to smell	The roses smell beautiful.
to sound	The music sounds strange.
to taste	The meat tastes awful.
to turn	The milk turned sour.

Verben anstelle von Adverbien

to be fond of	*gern*	to happen to	*zufällig*
to be likely to	*wahrscheinlich*	to hope	*hoffentlich*
to be sorry	*leider*	to prefer	*lieber*
to be supposed to	*vermutlich*	to seem to	*anscheinend*
to go on	*weiter*	(I) used to	*früher*

"You're a very naughty girl, Sarah! Aren't you sorry you bit poor Uncle George?"
"Yes, I am! He tasted horrible!"

Übung 1

Bilde die Adverbien folgender Adjektive. Achte auf die Schreibweise.

1 good
2 beautiful
3 successful
4 pretty
5 noble
6 sure
7 true
8 entire
9 careless
10 full
11 easy
12 faithful
13 surprising
14 dry
15 sad
16 common
17 bad
18 immediate
19 comfortable
20 intelligent
21 usual
22 ridiculous
23 constant
24 unbearable
25 hurried
26 hasty
27 diligent
28 lucky
29 furious
30 high
31 happy
32 definite
33 simple
34 different

Übung 2

Übersetze die folgenden Sätze und drücke die hervorgehobenen Wörter durch Verben aus.

1 *(Hoffentlich)* wird er bald kommen.
2 *(Leider)* kann ich nicht rechtzeitig kommen.
3 Er las *(weiter).*
4 Sie trafen sich *(zufällig)* auf der Straße.
5 Er mag Bier *(lieber)* als Wein.
6 Er liest *(gern)* englische Bücher.
7 Er ist *(anscheinend)* nicht hier.
8 Mach *(weiter),* bitte.
9 Sie machten *(weiter),* obwohl sie kaum Zeit hatten.
10 *(Hoffentlich)* bist du mir nicht böse.
11 Sie war *(anscheinend)* nicht überzeugt von seinen Argumenten.
12 Unsere Nachbarn waren *(zufällig)* am gleichen Urlaubsort.
13 Sie fuhren *(lieber)* nach London als nach Paris.
14 *(Früher)* ging er öfter ins Theater.

Übung 3

Setze die richtigen Formen ein.

1 John was □ hurt when he heard the accusation against him. (deep)
2 This is a □ produced car. No wonder it is falling apart. (cheap)
3 He was not □ satisfied with the results of the exam. (complete)
4 His parents □ agreed with his wish to become a doctor. (full)
5 He watched them □ . (close)
6 You have sold your books far too □ . (expensive)
7 He tried □, but in vain. (hard)
8 Leave my office, please. This is □ the time to ask for more money. (hard)
9 It was □ cold last night. (bitter)
10 He tasted the wine □ . cautious
11 After the operation she slept □ all night. (sound)
12 Don't go too □ to the railing. (close)
13 The milk tasted □ because it had turned □ . (awful, sour)
14 The music isn't too □, is it? (loud)

15 The prisoners of war were □ guarded. (close)
16 He took the bad news □ . (light)
17 We found him □ asleep when we entered the room. (sound)
18 The young girls were □ dressed. (pretty)

Übung 4

Adjektiv oder Adverb? Setze die richtige Form der angegebenen Wörter ein.

just · good · right · deep · quick · bright · angry · close · wrong · short · dear · fair · tired · hard · bad

1 He was so □ in thought that he didn't notice my arrival.
2 She went □ through the papers as she didn't have much time.
3 He watched him □ while he repaired the engine.
4 Everything seemed to go □ and there were no problems.
5 The fire was burning □ .
6 He was so □ in debt that he couldn't repay a single penny.
7 The party went so □ that everybody left early.
8 If you want to play scrabble with us, you must play □ .
9 He returned to work □ after his holidays.
10 He loved his parents □ .
11 You should have a break. You've worked really □ recently.
12 How long have you been working? You look really □ .
13 The solution he found seems to be □ . I don't know where I went □ .
14 I can □ wait to congratulate him on his final exams.
15 He was furious and looked □ at me.
16 Some questions were so □ that he couldn't answer them.
17 She is doing so □ at school. She always gets good marks. She is a very □ child.
18 We're running □ of time. We must hurry up.
19 I must stop you □ here as there is no time left.
20 One should be □ and treat both sides objectively.

Übung 5

Setze die Adverbien und adverbialen Wendungen an die richtige Stelle innerhalb des Satzes.

1 He was forty years old when he got married. (almost)
2 He goes to school at 7 o'clock. (usually)
3 They fly to London for business reasons. (occasionally)
4 We are going to London. (next week)
5 He has been to the United States. (never)
6 The summer was warm. (this year, extremely)
7 We heard a loud crash. (all of a sudden)
8 He realized that he was on the wrong side of the road. (slowly)
9 My father comes home from work. (never, before 8 o'clock)
10 The policeman stopped the car. (immediately)
11 It's nine o'clock. (exactly)
12 Our little son goes to bed. (at 7 o'clock, always)
13 He didn't notice it. (perhaps)
14 They've visited us. (this year, several times)
15 Have you heard such a terrible thing? (ever)

4 Die Pronomen

A Die Personalpronomen

Subjektform	I	you	he	she	it	we	you	they	
Objektform	me	you	him	her	it	us	you	them	
„man"						we	you	they	one

Fehlerquellen im Bereich der Personalpronomen:

Wiedergabe des deutschen „es" durch:

he, she, they
bei vorher genannten Personen

Who is that boy/girl? He/She is my friend.
Who are those people? They are friends of ours.

it
bei Sachen und nicht genannten Personen

What is it? It's a cup.
Who was it? It was John and Mary.

it (is/was) . . . that/who
bei Hervorhebung des Subjekts oder Objekts

It was the dog that died.

there (is/are/was/were)
bei Hinweis auf ein folgendes Subjekt

There's no time left.

so
nach den Verben des Sagens, Denkens, Wünschens, Fürchtens

be afraid, believe, do, expect, hope, say, think
Is he better? We hope so.

Keine Wiedergabe des deutschen „es".

Ich kann's.	Can you swim? – Yes, I can.
Ich weiß es nicht.	Can he swim? – I don't know.
Es freut mich.	I am glad.
Es geht mir gut.	I am well/fine.
Es tut mir leid.	I am sorry.
Es macht mir Spaß, Englisch zu sprechen.	I like speaking English.
Aber: Es gefällt mir hier.	I like it here.

"They were obviously experts – they didn't take anything."

Übung 1

Ersetze das deutsche „es".

1 Sorry, *(es ist)* nobody at home.
2 *(Es ist mir)* extremely cold, so close the windows, please.
3 *(Es gefällt mir)* very much in London.
4 Who was it? – *(Es waren)* the children.
5 Who rang the bell? – *(Es war)* the milkman.
6 Is he better now? – I believe *(es).*
7 I hope the weather will clear up soon. – I hope *(es),* too.
8 Who are these girls? – *(Es sind)* my friends.
9 The summer is coming to an end, isn't it? – I am afraid *(es).*
10 Where is the post office? – *(Es ist)* further down the road.
11 *(Es war)* an opportunity I had to take advantage of.
12 You must be wrong. *(Es war)* not John, but Peter you saw last night.
13 I like *(es)* to spend Christmas at home with my family.
14 He is supposed to be an excellent musician. – Who said *(es)*?
15 Is he in London now? – I don't know *(es).*
16 Can you speak French? – Yes, I can *(es).*
17 Shall we walk or take the bus? – I'd prefer *(es)* to walk.
18 Has he decided to move? – Yes, I think *(es).*

B Die Possessivpronomen

adjektivisch	my	your	his	her	its	our	your	their
substantivisch	mine	yours	his	hers	its	ours	yours	theirs

Fehlerquellen im Bereich der Possessivpronomen:

Der adjektivische Gebrauch

Im Englischen steht das adjektivisch gebrauchte Possessivpronomen bei folgenden Wörtern/Wortfeldern, wenn es sich auf ein vorher genanntes Subjekt bezieht:

– Kleidungsstücke und Körperteile

He entered the room with his hands in his pockets.
Hold your tongue.

– Wörter wie **life, mind, death** u.a.

They made up their minds to leave.

Aber: She took him by the hand. (**the** *bezieht sich auf* **him**)
The boxer gave his opponent a blow on the head.
He pulled him by the arm.

Die Betonung des Objekts

– erfolgt bei besonderer Verstärkung der adjektivischen Possessivpronomen durch **own.**

I've got my own car.
He used his own pen.

– erfolgt beim unbestimmten Artikel, bei Zahlwörtern, **no** und anderen Bestimmungswörtern stets durch **of**-Fügung **(. . . of his own).**

I've got a car of my own.
He had five houses of his own.

Der substantivische Gebrauch

Das Possessivpronomen tritt mit **of** hinter das Substantiv, wenn vor diesem ein unbestimmter Artikel, ein Zahlwort oder ein Demonstrativpronomen steht.

A neighbour of mine is in hospital.
Three books of hers are on the list.
That friend of yours is very nice.

Übung 1

Setze das passende Possessivpronomen oder den bestimmten Artikel ein.

1 She carried her little boy in ☐ arms.
2 He shrugged ☐ shoulders and didn't say any more.
3 She took the boy by ☐ hand and left the room.
4 When she gets up, she always combs and brushes ☐ hair first.
5 The police grabbed him by ☐ arm.
6 He suddenly jumped to ☐ feet and rushed out.
7 He was in ☐ late forties when he got married.
8 He lost ☐ appetite when he saw how dirty the tables were.
9 She shook ☐ head and didn't know what to say.
10 Suddenly someone tapped him on ☐ shoulder.
11 Have you hurt ☐ knee?
12 Go and wash ☐ hands before you come to lunch.
13 Many people lost ☐ lives in the disaster.
14 It doesn't look nice if you keep ☐ hands in ☐ pockets.
15 The police shook ☐ heads when they came to the scene of the accident.
16 He couldn't make up ☐ mind what to do first.

"There goes a car with exactly the same number as ours."

Übung 2

Gebrauche **own** oder **of his/her ... own** zur besonderen Betonung des Objekts.

Beispiel: It was his **decision** and no one else's.
It was his **own decision** and no one else's.

1 The Prime Minister always travels in his **aeroplane.**
2 When they arrived, it was their wish to have a **house.**
3 My grandfather was the first to have a **car.**
4 I could not believe it till I saw it with my **eyes.**
5 We do not have a **garden,** only a small plot.

C Die Reflexivpronomen

myself	yourself	himself	herself	itself
ourselves	yourselves	themselves		oneself

Die Reflexivpronomen dienen zur Hervorhebung eines Subjekts oder Objekts, einer Person oder Sache.

Did you see the man yourself? Did you see the man himself?

Nach einem Verb + Präposition werden Reflexivpronomen verwendet, um das Subjekt hervorzuheben.

He spoke to himself.
She addressed the envelope to herself.
Look after yourself.
He sat by himself.

Sie entfallen nach Präpositionen, die auf eine Örtlichkeit oder eine Person verweisen.

She closed the door behind her. *(hinter sich)*
They put the child between them.
Did you take your dog with you?

Viele im Deutschen reflexiv gebrauchte Verben haben im Englischen kein Reflexivpronomen.

Hauptfehlerquelle:
apologize, approach, change, happen, lie down, long for, recollect, remember, sit down, wonder

Im Deutschen und Englischen reflexiv gebrauchte Verben sind u.a.

amuse, ask, blame, console, convince, enjoy, hurt, introduce, look after } **oneself**

Ist das Verhältnis eindeutig, kann das Reflexivpronomen entfallen u.a. bei: **behave, dress, wash.**

She always behaves at school.
I wash before I dress.

Übung 1

Setze das Reflexivpronomen ein, wo nötig.

1 Don't forget to look after ☐ when you are so far away from home.
2 The children enjoyed ☐ immensely.
3 He usually shaves ☐, but today his wife had to help because he had injured his hand.
4 She often asked ☐ how this could have happened.
5 The children amused ☐ yesterday.
6 He remembered ☐ that it had been his fault.
7 Have you hurt ☐ ?
8 He lay ☐ down and had a rest.
9 He blamed ☐ for the accident as he had not been paying attention.
10 She introduced ☐ to the audience before her speech.
11 Why did you apologize ☐ for something you did not do?

D Die reziproken Pronomen

each other one another

Die reziproken Pronomen dienen zur Betonung der Wechselseitigkeit eines Geschehens.	They greeted each other/one another.	Sie begrüßten sich.
Fehlerquellen im Bereich der reziproken Pronomen:	They saw one another.	*Sie sahen sich = standen sich gegenüber*
	They saw themselves.	*Sie sahen sich = z.B. in einem Spiegel*

Übung 1

Reflexivpronomen oder reziprokes Pronomen?
Setze das passende ein.

1 They quarrelled among ☐ .
2 The two friends had not seen ☐ for years, but still liked ☐ .
3 We have known ☐ for a long time.
4 They kissed ☐ during the ceremony.
5 She looked at ☐ in the mirror.
6 John and Anne are very fond of ☐ and spend a lot of time together.
7 They got to know ☐ two years before they got married.
8 Try to look at ☐ before you blame other people.

E Die Demonstrativpronomen

adjektivisch und substantivisch

this — that — these — those

Der adjektivische Gebrauch

This exercise is easy.
These apples are good.
That answer is right.
Those jeans are expensive.

Der substantivische Gebrauch

This is impossible.
Do you want these?
I like that.
Those are too big.

This/These deuten auf etwas Näherliegendes.

What's this (here) on the table?

That/Those deuten auf etwas Entfernteres hin.

Can you give me that pencil (over there)?

Sie zeigen auch einen Gegensatz oder eine Auswahl an.

Do you prefer this skirt or that one?
Do you want these or those?

Beide Formen sind verwendbar, wenn auf etwas schon Erwähntes hingewiesen wird.

This/That is exactly what I mean.
These/Those are perfect.

Redewendungen

this morning
this month/year
that's it
that won't do
that's all right

Übung 1

Setze das entsprechende Demonstrativpronomen ein.

1 What a lovely day □ is.
2 Would you like □ shirt or □ one?
3 □ car here belongs to me.
4 I told you not to use □ typewriter, but □ one over there.
5 □ is the most exciting holiday I have ever had.
6 Which way shall I go – □ way or □ way?
7 □ were the days when we were young.
8 Where have you been □ summer?
9 □ month we have not been very successful.
10 I am not sure who □ papers here belong to.
11 Isn't □ your book over there?
12 □ cassettes over there are mine, too.

F Die Interrogativpronomen

substantivisch

Subjektform	Who	Whose	What	Which
Objektform	Who(m)	Whose	What	Which
adjektivisch	Whose	What	Which	

Der substantivische Gebrauch

als Subjekt
Gefragt wird mit **who, whose** nach Personen; mit **which** nach einer Person/Sache aus einer begrenzten Zahl und mit **what** nach Gegenständen.

Who is it?	It's Jane.
Whose is it?	It's Jane's.
Which is it?	It's the book on the left.
What is it?	It's a new machine.

als Objekt
Whom ist die Objektform von **who**.

Who(m) did they invite?

Immer häufiger ersetzt **who** die Form **whom** als Objektform.

To whom should I refer the matter?
Who should I refer the matter to?

Der adjektivische Gebrauch

Whose wird benutzt, wenn nach Besitz gefragt wird.

Whose car is parked in my parking place?
Jane's (car) is.

Ist die Auswahl nicht begrenzt oder wird nach der Beschaffenheit von Personen oder Sachen gefragt, wird **what** benutzt.

What countries have you visited?
What colour is your car?
What films do you like?

What {
do you call this?
is the English word for . . . ?
time is it?
sort of teacher is she?

Ist die Auswahl begrenzt, wird **which** verwendet.

Which country did you visit last?
Which colour do you prefer, pink or green?

Übung 1

Setze die richtigen Interrogativpronomen ein.

1 ☐ is he called?
2 ☐ river flows through Paris?
3 ☐ car is this? – A Rolls Royce.
4 ☐ of these flowers do you like best?
5 ☐ is he excited about? – His birthday.
6 ☐ have you decided to do?
7 ☐ is the longest river – the Thames, the Amazon or the Nile?
8 ☐ is afraid of Virginia Wolfe?
9 ☐ is the English word for 'klein'?
10 ☐ book is this? – Mine.
11 ☐ century is called 'The Age of Industrialization'?
12 ☐ is that woman?
13 ☐ are you going to the theatre with?
14 ☐ part of town would you like to live in?
15 ☐ of you came first?
16 ☐ colour are her eyes?
17 ☐ did you meet last night?
18 ☐ shall I give this to?
19 ☐ is 'groß' in English?
20 ☐ book is this – yours or his?

G Die Relativpronomen

who (whom) whose which that

Die Relativpronomen in bezug auf:

Personen	who	The young man who came in was her brother.
	who(m)	The young man [who(m)] I saw was her brother.
	whose	The young man whose brother came in was happy.
Sachen und ganze Sätze	which	She did what she could, which wasn't very much.
Personen und Sachen	that	He is the man that I like.
		It is the answer that I gave.

Am wichtigsten ist der Unterschied zwischen notwendigen und nicht-notwendigen Relativsätzen, der häufig zu Fehlern führt. Eine Trennungslinie ist nicht immer leicht zu ziehen, da es oft auf die Situation ankommt.

Notwendige Relativsätze

Ein notwendiger Relativsatz enthält Informationen, die für den Hauptsatz unentbehrlich sind. Kein Komma!

The people that/who noticed the fire left the room.
(nur diese, aber nicht alle)
The fastest car that I have ever driven is a Jaguar.
(von allen Autos, die ich gefahren habe)

!n einem notwendigen Relativsatz kann das Pronomen wegfallen, wenn es Objekt ist.

The man (that/who/whom) we met was my uncle.

Das Pronomen kann aber nicht wegfallen, wenn es Subjekt ist.

He's the man that/who wanted to see me.

In einem notwendigen Relativsatz mit **that** werden Präpositionen stets nachgestellt.

This is the woman (that) I sold the car to.

In einem notwendigen Relativsatz mit **who(m)/which** können Präpositionen vor dem Pronomen stehen.

He is the man in who(m) I put all my trust.
Here is the restaurant in which we ate.

Im Umgangsenglisch werden die Präpositionen vorzugsweise ans Ende gestellt.

He is the man (who) I put all my trust in.
Here is the restaurant (which) we ate in.

Nicht-notwendige Relativsätze

Ein nicht-notwendiger Relativsatz enthält lediglich zusätzliche Informationen, die für den Hauptsatz entbehrlich sind. Diese zusätzlichen Informationen werden durch Kommas abgehoben.

The people, who noticed the fire, left the room.
(alle, weil sie die Gefahr erkannten)

"Mary, the people with whom we exchanged addresses during our holiday are here."

Übung 1

Kombiniere die folgenden Sätze und verwende die entsprechenden Relativpronomen, wo erforderlich.

Beispiel: The brochures are very interesting. They are over there.
The brochures which are over there are very interesting.

1 George Orwell is a famous writer. I find his books highly interesting.
2 Did you like the book? I gave it to you yesterday.
3 He is the man. I put all my trust in him.
4 Who is the gentleman? You were talking to him.
5 This is not the same coat. You wore it yesterday.
6 This is Mr Smith. I'm looking after his dog when he's on holiday.
7 I've found the purse. I had lost it some time ago.
8 She is an artist from the United States. Her paintings are on exhibition in our town.
9 He wrote numerous books. They deal with modern history.

Übung 2

Ergänze die fehlenden Relativpronomen, wo nötig.

1 The girl ☐ you see over there is my sister.
2 The poet ☐ work is considered best will receive an award.
3 The car ☐ he had seen in the showroom was too expensive.
4 The people ☐ we met on our holiday visited us last week.
5 The boy ☐ I met in France is now living in America.
6 What do you think of the book ☐ I gave you for your birthday?
7 The vocabulary test ☐ we did yesterday was very difficult.
8 The flowers ☐ are blooming in our garden at the moment are all presents from our friends.
9 The trip ☐ my parents have booked for us this summer is very expensive.
10 What do you think of the people ☐ live next door?
11 Is your brother the boy ☐ had an accident on his bike last week?
12 The children were afraid of the ghosts ☐ haunted the old castle.
13 What do you think of the new book ☐ we are using in our English lessons?
14 Are you worried about the exam ☐ you took last week?
15 Twinned towns are usually places ☐ have similarities.
16 Russian is a language ☐ is very difficult to learn.
17 This is a factory ☐ employs many young people.
18 Mr Jones ☐ article was published in a leading newspaper works at our firm.
19 The cat ☐ had been living with us for ages was run over.
20 The number of people ☐ are killed on the roads is constantly increasing.

H Die indefiniten Pronomen

adjektivisch und substantivisch	some (a) few both	any each all	much (n)either *(Zahlwörter)*	many one another (a) little
adjektivisch	no	every	other	whole
substantivisch	none	others	some/any	

Die wichtigsten indefiniten Pronomen, bei denen oft Fehler gemacht werden:

some(-thing, -body, -one)
any(-thing, -body, -one)

Die Grundbedeutung beider Pronomen ist „etwas, ein paar, einige", und sie können als Adjektive oder Substantive gebraucht werden.

Adjektiv	**Substantiv**
Some books are easy to read.	I saw some on your bookshelf.
Do you have any English books?	There aren't any in this shop.

some

Bei **some** ist das „Etwas" tatsächlich vorhanden oder erreichbar.

Somebody is knocking at the door.

Some kommt in Fragesätzen beim Bitten oder Anbieten vor.

Would you like to have some more tea?
Could I have some of these, please?

any

Bei **any** ist das „Etwas" weder vorhanden noch erreichbar.

I didn't see anybody on the street.

Any steht oft in Frage-, Bedingungs- und Verneinungssätzen.

Have you got any money? If I had any, I would give it to you.
There aren't any trees in your garden and there aren't any in mine, either.

Aber: **Any** in bejahenden Sätzen bedeutet „jeder beliebige".

Take any flowers you want.

Weitere indefinite Pronomen

each

jeder einzelne

als Substantiv: Each of the students answered a question.
als Adjektiv: Each student thought he or she was right.

every
every: nur als Adjektiv;
als Substantiv: **everybody, everything, everyone**

jeder; alle
Christmas comes every year.
Everyone was there.

Redewendungen

every day/night/month	*jeden Tag/jede Nacht/jeden Monat*
every other day	*jeden zweiten Tag*
every two weeks	*alle zwei Wochen*
every now and then	*dann und wann*

Bei einer **of**-Fügung stets **each**.
each of us

much
viel
als Adjektiv — I didn't have much luck in the game.
als Substantiv — Much has been said about this problem.
In bejahenden Sätzen kann **a lot of, plenty of, a great deal of** anstelle von **much/many** stehen. — A lot of things have been said about this problem.

many
viele
als Adjektiv — He has not got many books.
als Substantiv — Many (of them) are too difficult to read.

either
jeder von beiden; der eine oder der andere
als Adjektiv — There was a lamp post on either side of the road.
als Substantiv — Do you want this or that? I'll take either.

neither
keiner von beiden; weder der eine noch der andere
als Adjektiv — Neither boy liked the work.
als Substantiv — Neither could come.

Aber: None could come. *Keiner (von allen) konnte kommen.*

little
wenig
als Adjektiv — Little food is left.
als Substantiv — Little is left.

(a) little
ein wenig
als Adjektiv — A little food is left.
als Substantiv — A little is left.

few
wenige
als Adjektiv — Few friends came to his party.
als Substantiv — Many were invited, but few came.

(a) few
ein paar; einige
als Adjektiv — A few drops of milk make all the difference.
als Substantiv — A few (of the students) understood the problem.

Übung 1

Setze ein: **some, any, somebody** oder **anybody**.

1 I remember having seen ☐ documents.
2 Is there ☐ at home?
3 If you have ☐ questions, do not hesitate to ask.
4 I saw ☐ beautiful flowers in your garden.
5 I could not find ☐ mistakes in your test.
6 Does ☐ know where she is?
7 She wanted ☐ bread, but there was not ☐ left at the baker's.
8 At the end of the talk he asked if there were ☐ questions.
9 Hardly ☐ knew what was to be done next.
10 I am sorry I cannot help you. Ask ☐ else, please.
11 This soup is delicious! Can I have ☐ more, please?
12 Listen! I heard a funny noise. I am sure there is ☐ upstairs.

Übung 2

Setze die entsprechenden Pronomen ein.

a little · little · few · a few · much · many

1 We have been living here for quite ☐ years now.
2 We still have ☐ time left. So, we could talk it over.
3 He is extremely busy and doesn't have ☐ time for his favourite kind of sport.
4 Very ☐ people understand Einstein's theory of relativity.
5 Although they have been living here for ☐ years now, they haven't made ☐ friends.
6 There's not ☐ time left for you to do what you have been asked.
7 They have been away for ☐ days now and we expect them back tomorrow.
8 So ☐ the better.
9 He asked her if she liked him at least ☐ .
10 The road was lit; so we had ☐ trouble finding the right house.
11 He couldn't speak English; so he understood ☐ of what she tried to explain.
12 He understood only ☐ French words.
13 She sent her boy to the baker's to buy ☐ rolls.
14 Go on, take as ☐ fruit as you like.
15 There is ☐ hope that the shipwrecked people can be saved.

Übung 3

Setze die entsprechenden Pronomen ein.

each · every · either · neither · everything

1 ☐ member of the staff had to come to the conference.
2 There was a radio in ☐ hotel room.
3 There was a meeting ☐ other week.
4 There were houses on ☐ side of the road.
5 I see her ☐ now and then.
6 ☐ of us could go to the party as we were both ill.
7 ☐ young man has to join the army for a certain length of time.
8 Which of the two pullovers would suit you better? You can have ☐ .
9 She has ☐ the wish nor the financial means to help him.
10 I was quite honest and told him ☐ .

"There must be something out there you haven't vandalized."

Übung 4

Lies und versuche zu verstehen!

One day SOMEBODY said to EVERYBODY: NOBODY does ANYTHING. We can't let EVERYONE hang around EVERYWHERE doing nothing. SOMEONE must start doing SOMETHING. Now EVERYBODY was looking EVERYWHERE to find SOMEBODY to start to do SOMETHING. EVERYONE thought if SOMETHING happened, EVERYTHING would be o.k., anyway. But the consequence was that EVERYONE is still waiting today for SOMETHING to happen or SOMEBODY to do SOMETHING. To cut it short: NOBODY does ANYTHING!

5 Das Verb

A Die modalen Hilfsverben

can	may	shall	will	ought to
could	might	should	would	must, need

Die modalen Hilfsverben können weder den Infinitiv noch Partizipien bilden. Bei ihnen ist folgendes zu beachten:

In der 3. Person Singular (Gegenwart) haben sie kein **-s**.

She can read. He must go.

Die Frage- und Verneinungsformen werden ohne **to do** gebildet.

Can she read? No, she can't.
Would he go if he could? No, he wouldn't.

Verben wie **can, may, must** müssen durch andere Verben ersetzt werden, wenn sie nicht in der Gegenwart stehen.

I can come now.	I will be able to help you next weekend.
You may smoke here.	The children weren't allowed to watch TV yesterday.
She must finish her homework before dinner.	We have never had to learn so much for a test before.

Die modalen Hilfsverben können unter anderem folgendes ausdrücken:

Fähigkeit/Können
can, could

I can read Russian, but I cannot speak it.
John could talk at an early age.

Statt **could** wird **to be able to** gebraucht, um die Fähigkeit und eine besondere Handlung in der Vergangenheit auszudrücken. **Was/were able to** ist immer dann richtig, wenn man statt dessen auch **managed to** verwenden kann. In Fragen und verneinten Sätzen kann **could** immer verwendet werden.

The doctor was able to help him after the accident.
The rescuers were able to reach the exhausted swimmer in time.
John was able to save enough money for his bicycle trip.

Erlaubnis
can, could, may

Can I come in?
(*Höflicher:* Could/May I come in?)

Statt **can, could, may** werden **to be allowed to, to be permitted** to als Ersatzformen verwendet.

The children were allowed to stay up late on Saturdays.
The prisoners were permitted to take two hours' exercise a day.

Vermutung, Wahrscheinlichkeit, denkbare Möglichkeit
may, might

It may rain tonight. *(wahrscheinlich)*
It might rain tonight. *(möglich)*

Notwendigkeit, Verpflichtung
must (in der Gegenwart)

You must come at once.

have to vertritt **must** in allen anderen Zeiten, ist aber auch in der Gegenwart gebräuchlich.

You don't have to come at once.
You didn't have to come yesterday.

Nicht-Notwendigkeit
need (not)
don't/didn't have to kann auch **need (not)** vertreten.

There is no school on Sundays; you don't have to go.
We needn't worry about the crew. They have just phoned to say they are safe.

striktes Verbot
mustn't

You mustn't smoke here.
People must not enter this area without permission.

Ermahnung, Ratschlag
should

You should go and see him.
You shouldn't drink so much.

ought to (stärker als **should**)

You ought to help him with his work.

Bitte, Absicht, Vorsatz, Entschlossenheit
will/shall

Will you help me, please?
I shall ask him.

would (bei dringendem Wunsch und in verneinten Sätzen)

He wouldn't listen to her.

Bitte, Aufforderung, Wunsch
would

Would you go on reading, please?

gewohnheitsmäßige Handlung, typisches Verhalten
will, would

Boys will be boys.
She would read fairy tales every night.

In den folgenden Übungen werden einige besonders fehlerträchtige Punkte bei den modalen Hilfsverben berücksichtigt.

Übung 1

Setze die richtigen Formen ein.

1 Children □ be careful when crossing the road. (must/may)
2 You □ trespass beyond this point. (mustn't/wouldn't)
3 This is, if I □ say so, the truth. (may/can)

4 You □ smoke near a petrol station. (mustn't/needn't)
5 □ you lend me a ruler? (can/must)
6 Young children □ always offer their seats to elderly people. (should/might)
7 It's a pity that you □ come. (cannot/needn't)
8 □ you speak English? (can/may)
9 My aunt □ sit in front of the fireplace every evening. (should/would)
10 You □ drink and drive. (mustn't/needn't)

Übung 2

Übersetze die folgenden Sätze.

1 Wir konnten nicht kommen.
2 Er durfte nicht Fußball spielen.
3 Darf ich jetzt gehen?
4 Er könnte das bestimmt tun.
5 Wir besuchten unsere Großeltern jedes Weihnachten.
6 Könntest du nicht etwas höflicher sein?
7 Sie mußten sehr schwer arbeiten.
8 Dieses Problem können wir einfach nicht lösen.
9 Das kannst du schaffen, wenn du dich bemühst.
10 Sie dürfen hier nicht rauchen.

Übung 3

Bilde richtige Sätze.

Beispiel: 1 John has trouble reading the blackboard. He really must wear glasses.

1 John has trouble reading the blackboard. He really. . .	may	rain later.
2 Take your umbrella. It . . .	can	come any time you like.
3 When she was younger she . . .	must	wear glasses.
4 You . . .	shouldn't	do much homework.
5 When I was at school I . . .	need	spend hours reading. Now she has no time.
6 She is not clever enough. So, I . . .	didn't have to	all the money myself.
7 I cannot give you any financial help. I . . .	would	help her.
8 The film is terrible. Children . . .	ought to	see it.

Übung 4

Setze ein: **mustn't** oder **needn't**.

1 You ☐ learn the whole poem. It's far too long.
2 You ☐ drive so fast when there are children around.
3 I ☐ forget to remind him about the meeting.
4 I'm sure it won't rain. You ☐ take an umbrella.
5 You've given me too many potatoes. – You ☐ eat them all.
6 You ☐ make so much noise. It's very late.
7 When you go abroad you ☐ forget your passport.
8 You ☐ enter a one-way street from the wrong direction.

Übung 5

Beende die folgenden Sätze.

1	He must be a good teacher, . . .	**A**	can't you?
2	You can speak English, . . .	**B**	mustn't we?
3	We must be tolerant, . . .	**C**	should he?
4	I can believe you, . . .	**D**	can you?
5	We might be able to help you, . . .	**E**	will you?
6	He should drive carefully, . . .	**F**	shouldn't he?
7	We should help him, . . .	**G**	can't I?
8	You can't help me, . . .	**H**	mustn't he?
9	He shouldn't talk so badly about his friends, . . .	**I**	mightn't we?
10	You won't forget to do the shopping, . . .	**J**	shouldn't we?

Übung 6

Setze die englische Entsprechung der deutschen Wörter in die Lücken ein und übersetze anschließend den ganzen Satz.

1 We ☐ wait for half an hour yesterday. *(müssen)*
2 You ☐ eat any more if you are not hungry. *(nicht brauchen)*
3 If he asks us politely, we ☐ help him. *(müssen)*
4 You ☐ talk such nonsense. *(nicht sollen)*
5 ☐ I see you again soon? *(dürfen)*
6 Things like that ☐ easily happen. *(können)*
7 It ☐ turn misty at night. *(können)*
8 I ☐ work any overtime last month. *(nicht müssen)*
9 I think you ☐ work a bit harder. *(sollen)*
10 You ☐ make an appointment, but it's probably better to. *(nicht brauchen)*

Übung 7

Entscheide: **could** oder **was/were able to**.

1 They ☐ save enough money for their last holidays.
2 He ☐ play the guitar very well when he was only six.
3 My bike was broken yesterday, but my father ☐ repair it.
4 We ☐ talk about it when we met yesterday.
5 My parents ☐ catch the plane although the car broke down on the way to the airport.
6 She ☐ escape although the gangster held her firmly.
7 We ☐ only use the downstairs room because the roof was broken.

B Der Gebrauch der Zeiten

Die Zeiten der Gegenwart

Die Verlaufsform (present continuous)

Die Verlaufsform drückt u.a. aus, daß:

- etwas im gegenwärtigen Augenblick oder Zeitraum vor sich geht (oft in Verbindung mit **at the moment, just, now**).

  I'm just watching an interesting documentary on TV.
  I'm writing a book this summer.

- zwei oder mehr Handlungen sich zur gleichen Zeit abspielen.

  He is cleaning the dining room and she is doing the dishes.

- etwas zu einem bestimmten Zeitpunkt in der Zukunft geschehen wird.

  I'm meeting him tomorrow/tonight/next Sunday.

- eine Handlung sich häufig wiederholt oder andauert und mißbilligt wird (in Verbindung mit **always** oder **forever**).

  He is always forgetting his book.
  She is forever working.

Die einfache Form (simple present)

Die einfache Form wird u.a. benutzt bei:

- gewohnheitsmäßigen Handlungen (oft in Verbindung mit **never, always, every day, often, rarely, usually**).

She speaks English with her teacher.
Betty always travels abroad during her summer holidays.

- der Angabe von beruflichen Aktivitäten, Fähigkeiten oder allgemeinen Tatsachen.

He works at a garage.
She plays the guitar excellently.
The sun rises in the east.

- Verben des Sagens **(say, answer, ask)** sowie bei der Angabe von Handlungsfolgen (z.B. bei der Kommentierung von Sportereignissen) und bei Inhaltsangaben.

He says that he cannot tell me.
We leave at 10 am and arrive at 11 am.
He kicks the ball and scores!
In chapter one he loses his job. In chapter two he decides to go abroad. In chapter three . . .

Verben, die keine Handlung ausdrücken, sondern Meinungen, Gefühle (Abneigung, Liebe usw.), stehen in der Regel nur in der einfachen Form.

(dis)agree, (dis)like, forget, hate, know, love, mean, mind, refuse, remember, suppose, think, understand, want, wish

Dazu gehören auch:

- Verben der Sinneswahrnehmung

feel, hear, look, notice, see, smell, taste

- Verben, die Besitzverhältnisse ausdrücken

belong, consist, contain, have, own, possess

Verben wie **have, look** oder **think** können in der Verlaufsform gebraucht werden, wenn sie keinen Zustand, sondern eine Tätigkeit ausdrücken.

We're having dinner.
What are you thinking of?
I'm seeing him tomorrow.
The cook is tasting/smelling the soup.

Übung 1

Setze ein: einfache Form oder Verlaufsform der Gegenwart.

1 I □ (usually/walk) to school.
2 He □ (write) a book at the moment.
3 My father □ (smoke) too much.
4 They □ (have) a beautiful house in which we □ (often/spend) our summer holidays.
5 Who is that gentleman? □ (you/know) him?
6 My uncle is very good at languages. He □ (speak) five.
7 He □ (often/go) to his club, but this evening he □ (visit) his aunt.
8 □ (you/understand) what he □ (say)?
9 □ (you/mind) explaining again what you □ (mean)?
10 Don't disturb me, please. I □ (watch) an interesting programme on TV.
11 It □ (smell) terrible outside. Close the window, please.
12 I □ (have) a problem. I □ (think) of moving house, but I □ (not/know) where to go.
13 I □ (get up) at 7 o'clock, □ (have) breakfast and □ (go) to school about an hour later.
14 He □ (work) in a factory which □ (produce) bicycles.
15 Hallo, John. What □ (you/do) here? – I □ (wait) for my bus.
16 They □ (pack) their suitcases because they □ (want) to go away tomorrow.
17 He □ (hate) writing letters.
18 Don't go out. It □ (pour) with rain.
19 The parcel □ (contain) a lot of sweets.
20 He cannot answer the phone because he □ (have) a shower.
21 Our friends □ (live) in London, but at the moment they □ (stay) in Manchester.
22 Reporter: John □ (kick) the ball to Peter, Peter □ (beat) one defender, □ (pass) the ball to Charles and he □ (score) a goal.

Die Vergangenheit

Die Verlaufsform (past continuous)

Die Verlaufsform wird gebraucht, um auszudrücken, daß eine Handlung (Verlaufsform) in der Vergangenheit durch ein neues Ereignis (einfache Form) unterbrochen wird.

While I was watching an interesting programme, my father entered the room.
I was walking along the street when I saw her at the bus-stop.
He was papering the dining room when he heard a strange noise in the kitchen.

Die Verlaufsform kann ferner gebraucht werden, um den Verlauf einer Handlung besonders zu betonen.

What were you doing yesterday at 8 o'clock? I tried to phone you. – I was having a bath.
While I was cleaning the garage, my father was washing our car.

Die einfache Form (simple past)

Mit der einfachen Form kann man ausdrücken, daß:

– ein Vorgang als abgeschlossen gilt (oft in Verbindung mit Zeitbestimmungen wie **yesterday, four years ago, last week** usw.).

Yesterday, I washed my car.
We visited London last year.
He bought a new pair of shoes at the weekend.

– mehrere Handlungen aufeinander folgten.

He knocked at the door, entered the room, and sat down.

Übung 1

Setze ein: einfache Form oder Verlaufsform der Vergangenheit.

1 We □ (meet) them a few years ago.
2 Before she □ (go) to the cinema, she □ (have) a shower, □ (wash) her hair and □ (dress) nicely.
3 Why □ (you/not/come)? – It □ (rain) cats and dogs, so I □ (think) I'd better stay at home.
4 Shakespeare □ (write) numerous dramas.
5 Where □ (you/meet) him? I □ (meet) him at the theatre.
6 My friend □ (visit) us several times last month.
7 My mother □ (just/prepare) dinner when our neighbour □ (knock) at the door and □ (ask) for a few eggs.
8 What □ (you/think) of his latest piece of art? – I □ (like) it very much.
9 "What □ (you/do) at 10 am?" the policeman □ (ask) the suspect.
10 When I □ (come) in at 8 o'clock he □ (watch) TV.
11 As a teenager he □ (play) the guitar.
12 I suddenly □ (remember) the contents of the novel as he □ (talk) about it.
13 Last year he □ (inherit) a lot of money and soon □ (own) a considerable amount of property.
14 When I □ (look) out of the window this morning it □ (rain).
15 What time □ (they/arrive)?

Das Perfekt

Der Gebrauch der Vergangenheit und des Perfekts **(present perfect)** ist im Englischen strengen Regeln unterworfen, während im Deutschen beide Zeiten nebeneinander gebraucht werden.

Das englische Perfekt drückt aus, daß eine in der Vergangenheit begonnene Handlung mit der Gegenwart in Verbindung steht, d.h. das Ergebnis noch sichtbar ist; oft in Verbindung mit Ausdrücken wie **up to now, so far, (not)** . . . **yet, just, ever, this year, today, already, never**.

Die Vergangenheit dagegen bezeichnet eine Handlung, die schon beendet wurde und keinerlei Verbindung zur Gegenwart mehr hat; oft in Verbindung mit **yesterday, last night, a minute ago**.

Das Perfekt (present perfect)
Die einfache Form wird gebraucht bei:

– Handlungen, die gerade abgeschlossen wurden.

I have just finished a letter to my son.

– Handlungen, die zwar in der Vergangenheit abgeschlossen wurden, aber durch keine Zeitbestimmung näher bestimmt sind.

I've read that book three times.
Have you ever been to London?

– Handlungen, die in der Vergangenheit begonnen haben, aber noch nicht abgeschlossen sind.

I have known him for three years now.

Zu besonders vielen Fehlern verleitet das englische Perfekt in Verbindung mit **since** und **for**, die im Deutschen beide mit „seit" wiedergegeben werden. Der entsprechende Satz steht im Deutschen in der Gegenwart.

Ich kenne ihn seit 3 Monaten.	=	I have known him for 3 months. *(Zeitraum)*
Ich kenne ihn seit Januar.	=	I have known him since January. *(Zeitpunkt)*

Übung 1

Entscheide: Vergangenheit oder Perfekt?

1 The plane from London □ (just/arrive).
2 □ (you/have) lunch yet? – Yes, I □ (have) lunch an hour ago.
3 Where □ (you/learn) your fluent French?
4 □ (you/see) any exciting films lately?
5 They □ (not/finish) building the factory yet.
6 I □ (buy) a new car last week, but I □ (not/sell) my old one yet.
7 I can't find my car key. □ (you/see) it anywhere?
8 I □ (not/see) him for some time. □ (you/hear) from him? – Yes, I □ (get) a letter yesterday.
9 □ (you/be) to the theatre lately? – Yes, I □ (see) Shaw's 'Arms and the Man' last Saturday.
10 □ (you/ever/be) to Edinburgh? – Yes, I □ (go) there for the festival last year.
11 During the last few weeks prices □ (go up).
12 When □ (you/born)?
13 What time □ (you/get up) this morning?
14 □ (you/see) her about the book this week? – No, I □ (not/talk) to her about it yet.
15 I □ (not/speak) to him before.
16 He □ (travel) a lot when he □ (be) younger.
17 We □ (see) them several times this year.
18 He □ (already/visit) us twice.
19 He □ (go) to America five years ago and □ (be) there ever since.
20 The Spaniards □ (conquer) South America.

Übung 2

Setze ein: **since** oder **for**.

1 A lot of things have changed □ I was a boy.
2 I've been trying to explain what I mean □ half an hour.
3 They have had rain □ the day before yesterday.
4 My father has been a member of the chess club □ several years.
5 The workers have been on strike □ last Monday.
6 The country has developed enormously □ the end of the war.
7 I have not seen them □ years.
8 It has been a long time □ I saw you last.
9 A lot of people have visited the exhibition □ it opened last week.
10 He has been unemployed □ five months now.
11 She has not had an accident □ she bought her car.
12 I haven't played football □ I was hurt in a game.
13 I haven't been here □ ages.
14 The house hasn't been lived in □ the last five years.
15 She has not been back here □ she was born.

Die Zukunft

Es gibt mehrere Formen, deren Verwendung von der Sprechabsicht abhängt.

Das **will-future** wird verwendet:

- bei Vorhersagen über künftige Ereignisse, auf die man keinen Einfluß hat.

  He will be 16 next week.

- nach Verben in der Gegenwart wie **be afraid, be sure, expect, hope, promise, suppose, think.**

  I expect we will see him there.

- bei spontanen Entschlüssen oder Reaktionen.

  Trust me, I'll help you.

Ich will dir helfen.	=	I want to help you.
Ich werde dir helfen.	=	I will help you.

Weitere Formen der Zukunft:

Die Verlaufsform der Gegenwart

bei festen Plänen (oft in Verbindung mit Zeitadverbien wie **tomorrow, next week** usw.).

We're travelling to Italy next week.
(We already have our tickets.)

Going to-future

bei einer festen Absicht.

I've just bought a typewriter. I'm going to learn to type.

Die einfache Gegenwart

bei Ereignissen, die nicht beeinflußbar sind und vom Kalender, Fahrplänen usw. abhängen.

The train leaves at six o'clock.

Übung 1

Verlaufsform der Gegenwart oder **will-future?**

1 They ☐ (travel) to Scotland this summer.
2 He ☐ (visit) his grandparents next week.
3 He has to work harder or he ☐ (fail) his exams.
4 I don't think I ☐ (recognize) him.
5 My father and brother ☐ (play) golf tomorrow.
6 She ☐ (be) sixteen next month.
7 I can't speak English, so my son ☐ (talk) to you.
8 The grass ☐ (grow) again when it rains.
9 They ☐ (get married) in October.
10 I'm sure that he ☐ (like) the arrangements.

Übung 2

Zukunft mit **going to** oder **will?**

1 We ☐ (travel) to England for our summer holiday.
2 I don't understand this. – Don't worry. I ☐ (come) and show you how to do it.
3 What about our trip to London? – Come for dinner this evening and we ☐ (talk) about it then.
4 I'm sure that they ☐ (see) the change when they come.
5 We all hope that he ☐ (be) in time for the race.
6 The weather forecast predicts that it ☐ (be) very warm tomorrow.
7 There is an interesting programme on TV this evening. ☐ (you/watch) it?
8 The police expect that the burglars ☐ (return) to the building.
9 I think that he ☐ (agree) with me.
10 I expect that we ☐ (spend) our next holiday skiing in the Alps.
11 It looks as if it ☐ (snow) tonight.
12 They are afraid that they ☐ (not have) enough time to do what he expects from them.
13 What are your brother's plans? ☐ (he/spend) a year in America?
14 My friend ☐ (visit) me when he is in London again.
15 I am sure the arrangement ☐ (not please) him at all.
16 They bought their tickets yesterday. They ☐ (take) the train because they hate flying.

Übung 3

Setze ein: Verlaufsform der Gegenwart oder einfache Gegenwart.

1 Winter ☐ (begin) on December 23rd.
2 I'm looking forward to this evening. I ☐ (take) my girl-friend to a restaurant.
3 The next plane for New York ☐ (leave) at 2.30 pm.
4 We ☐ (go) to the fair tomorrow.
5 The discussion programme ☐ (start) at 9 o'clock.
6 My cousin ☐ (come) next month.
7 The train from London ☐ (arrive) at 11 o'clock.
8 The liner ☐ (sail) next week.
9 They ☐ (leave) here at six and ☐ (catch) the early train from Paddington.
10 ☐ (you/walk) home this evening or ☐ (you/take) a taxi?

C Der Infinitiv

Eine weitere grammatische Form, bei deren Gebrauch oft Fehler gemacht werden, ist der Infinitiv. Seiner Bedeutung nach ist er unveränderbar und sagt nichts über die Person sowie die Zahl oder das Tempus aus. Der Infinitiv gehört – ebenso wie das Partizip und das Gerundium – zu den Satzmitteln, mit denen die englische Sprache Kürze und Straffung im Ausdruck erreicht.
Es ist häufig schwer zu bestimmen, wann der Infinitiv *mit* **to** oder *ohne* **to** gebraucht wird.

Mit 'to'

Der Infinitiv mit **to** steht:

- in der Regel nach Adjektiven (alle Steigerungsformen), Ordinalzahlen und **the only**. Statt des Infinitivs kann auch ein Relativsatz stehen.

It is better to tell the truth.
She was the second to arrive.
They were the only ones to visit me in hospital.
They were the only ones who visited me in hospital.

- nach Fragewörtern und **whether** in Verbindung mit Verben wie **ask, decide, forget, know, learn, remember, show, teach, tell, wonder**.

He told me how to get there.
He wanted to know whether to take his umbrella or not.

- nach **for** in Verbindung mit einem Substantiv oder Pronomen.

This job is too difficult for him to do.

- nach bestimmten Verben (u.a. **want/would like**) mit folgendem Objekt.

I want/would like you to be back at nine o'clock.

- nach Verben (+ Objekt), die ein Wollen, Wünschen oder deren Gegenteil ausdrücken sowie des Zulassens, Veranlassens oder Befehlens (u.a. **advise, allow, compel, encourage, expect, force, instruct, invite, order, permit, persuade, teach, tell, warn**).

They forced him to eat.
He taught her to speak English.
The teacher encouraged him to continue his studies.
He expected us to be home in time.
She told me not to be late.

Ohne 'to'

Der Infinitiv ohne **to** steht:

– nach allen Hilfsverben und Fügungen wie **had better, why not, would rather.**

He must come.
You'd better tell him everything.
Why not ask him for advice?

Aber: **ought to** ist eine feste Verbindung.

– nach den Verben **make** (veranlassen) sowie **to let** (zulassen).

Onions make your eyes water.
The teacher let us go home early.

– nach den Verben der sinnlichen Wahrnehmung (u.a. **feel, hear, notice, observe, see, watch**), wenn das Ende der Handlung besonders betont werden soll.

The police watched the thieves run away.

Übung 1

Entscheide: Infinitiv mit oder ohne **to**.

1 They made us □ (leave) the room.
2 She can □ (come) whenever she wants to.
3 You should □ (start) at once.
4 You ought □ (tell) the truth.
5 Where would you like □ (go) this evening?
6 If you wish, we could □ (go) to a concert.
7 His teacher let him □ (go) home before the bell rang.
8 It was not easy □ (find) a solution to the problem.
9 I would like him □ (go) to London to earn his living.
10 He advised us □ (follow) his orders.
11 My parents invited our guests □ (stay) as long as they wanted to.
12 He was the first □ (come) and the last □ (leave).
13 The minister wanted him □ (accept) his new post.
14 The team is expected □ (arrive) on Monday.
15 I couldn't □ (remember) what he said.
16 He should know what □ (do) under these circumstances.
17 It is very difficult □ (understand) what he means.
18 The nurse told the patient □ (be) more confident.
19 Why not □ (believe) him and □ (follow) his advice?
20 People are asked □ (not step) across the white line.
21 Would you like □ (join) our club?
22 It's better □ (leave) before the appointed time.
23 They'd better □ (stay) in as it is very cold outside.
24 The gangster instructed the bank manager □ (not inform) the police.
25 He wanted to know whether □ (bring) any money with him.
26 She forgot □ (ask) him for the travel brochure.

27 This problem is too difficult for him □ (understand).
28 The police couldn't let him □ (go) as he was still under suspicion.
29 Please tell the pupils □ (be) quieter.
30 We asked him □ (leave).
31 The police warned all the children □ (be) careful when crossing the road.
32 The local council invited a lot of firms □ (settle) in their town.
33 He asked his son □ (not buy) such a fast car.
34 She didn't know how □ (tell) him what had happened.
35 He warned them □ (not go), but they wouldn't listen.

Übung 2

Kombiniere beide Sätze. Benutze **for** + Objekt + Infinitiv.

Beispiel: This task was too difficult. He couldn't do it.
This task was too difficult for him to do.

1 Our new car was too fast. He didn't drive it.
2 She spoke loudly enough. Everybody could hear her.
3 The box was too heavy. The porter couldn't carry it.
4 It is impossible. I cannot do this test.
5 The text is too difficult. I cannot possibly translate it into German.
6 Is this dress cheap enough? Can you buy it?
7 It is important. They must leave early enough.
8 The house is not ready. They cannot move in yet.
9 The mountain is too high. We cannot climb it.
10 The summer in Italy is too hot. We shouldn't spend our holiday there.

Übung 3

Verwende die Infinitivkonstruktion nach bestimmten Verben.

Beispiel: He didn't allow □ (they come in).
He didn't allow them to come in.

1 She expected □ (the people listen to what she wanted).
2 Everybody expects □ (he does his duty).
3 His parents want □ (their son studies harder).
4 The teacher wants □ (the student is in time for his exam).
5 His father expects □ (he passes his driving test).
6 The police advised □ (people are aware of pickpockets).
7 We all wanted □ (they lead a happy life).
8 I asked □ (he leaves the building).
9 Do you want □ (the children play outside)?
10 The minister preferred □ (his colleagues assemble in the conference room and not in the office).
11 We must encourage □ (our children have more self-confidence).
12 My brother persuaded □ (he stays longer).
13 We asked □ (they tell the police if they saw anything dangerous).

"I like to recreate their natural environment."

Übung 4

Verkürze die folgenden Sätze durch die Verwendung des Infinitivs.

Beispiel: There is nobody there who can give you money.
There is nobody there to give you money.

1 Here is a book which will help you in your studies.
2 I don't have any money left which I can give you.
3 We found a porter who could carry our suitcases.
4 In Scotland there are a lot of mountains which we can climb.
5 He was the best football player who had ever joined our club.
6 They were the first who arrived for the match.
7 Have you anything that you could give those poor people?
8 Have you anything that you ought to declare?
9 Can you tell us how we can get to Heathrow by bus?
10 The police didn't know whether they should go on watching the suspect or not.
11 The registrar explained to the young couple how they had to fill in the application form.
12 The burglar discovered how he could break into the house.
13 The prisoners found out how they could escape from their cells.
14 His son couldn't decide whether he should study medicine or philosophy.
15 The young boy was the only one who survived the disaster.
16 Columbus was thought to be the first European who stepped on American soil.
17 The captain was the last who left the ship.
18 It took him a long time to learn how he could drive a car.
19 The doctor didn't know how he could tell him the truth.
20 In the darkness they didn't know how they could get to the station.
21 She asked me who we should invite to our party.
22 I showed him how he could use the tools.

D Das Gerundium

Das Gerundium wird durch das Anfügen der Endung **-ing** an das Verb gebildet und hat substantivische Eigenschaften. Es kann als Subjekt oder Objekt verwendet werden.

I like swimming. Swimming is my favourite sport. We talked about swimming across the river.

Das Gerundium steht:

– nach formelhaften Wendungen wie **there is no . . . , I can't help . . . , it's worth . . . , how about . . . , to be near to . . . , to feel like . . .**

It's worth looking at it.
How about having lunch here?
I feel like sleeping now.

– nach bestimmten Adjektiven wie **afraid of, fond of.**

He's afraid of sleeping in the dark.
She's fond of reading aloud.

– nach bestimmten Verben wie **admit, avoid, delay, dislike, enjoy, fancy, finish, give up, imagine, mention, mind, postpone, suggest.**

You should avoid making mistakes.
She gave up smoking years ago.
I didn't mention seeing him.
They postponed taking their holiday for another week.

– nach Verben und Adjektiven, die eng mit einer Präposition verbunden sind u.a. **accuse of, apologize for, believe in, depend on, engaged in, insist on, keep from, look forward to, prevent from, responsible for, succeed in, thank for, think of, tired of.**

I insist on helping you.
I apologize for saying that.
I look forward to hearing from you.
Thank you for helping me.
He's tired of working.

als adverbiale Bestimmung:

– der Zeit nach **after, before, on**

After seeing the film, they left.

– des Grundes nach **for, from**

He was punished for being late.

– des Mittels nach **by, in**

He learned a lot by reading books.

– der Art und Weise nach **instead of, without**

He left without saying a word.

– der Einräumung nach **in spite of**

In spite of carefully planning the holiday, we didn't enjoy it.

Das Gerundium oder der Infinitiv

Bei einigen Verben sind sowohl das Gerundium als auch der Infinitiv möglich, u.a. **begin, start, cease, continue, intend.**
Nach Verben wie **hate, like, love** und **prefer** wird für den Einzelfall der Infinitiv, für eine allgemeine Feststellung das Gerundium bevorzugt.

I hate to interrupt you.	I hate doing homework.

Nach **forget, go on, mean, remember, regret, stop, try** usw. wird das Gerundium oder der Infinitiv je nach Bedeutung verwendet.

She remembered going there.	*sich an etwas erinnern*
She remembered to go there.	*sich erinnern, etwas zu tun*
She stopped seeing him.	*aufhören, etwas zu tun*
She stopped to have a look at the car.	*eine Pause machen*
He tried eating fish for breakfast.	*etwas ausprobieren*
He tried to go home early.	*sich bemühen, etwas zu tun*
He regrets doing that.	*etwas bereuen*
I regret to inform you that he is ill.	*etwas bedauern*
He went on reading.	*etwas weitermachen*
He went on to do his homework.	*etwas als nächstes tun*
They never forgot meeting the president.	*vergessen, daß man etwas getan hat*
They forgot to buy her a present.	*vergessen, etwas zu tun*
That means making more money.	*etwas bedeuten*
We mean to make the best of it.	*etwas beabsichtigen*

Übung 1

Das Gerundium nach bestimmten Präpositionen. Setze die richtigen Präpositionen ein.

1. You should always apologize ☐ being late.
2. He ought to be ashamed ☐ having lied to her.
3. The helpers were congratulated ☐ having helped in spite of the unpleasant conditions.
4. The sailors tried to keep their ship ☐ sinking by pumping the water out.
5. His grandfather was extremely fit because he always believed ☐ taking exercise.

6 I'm looking forward □ meeting them.
7 The storm prevented us □ leaving.
8 The detective has eventually succeeded □ finding the murderer.
9 My friend thanked him □ helping him finish his book.
10 The shop assistant accused the young boy □ having stolen a few bottles of milk.
11 The scouts are thinking □ spending their holidays in Wales this summer.
12 Their teacher was tired □ explaining the same thing again and again.
13 The speaker objected □ being interrupted in the middle of his speech.
14 Your plan might not materialize; so don't rely □ earning a lot of money.
15 The secret police seem to delight □ torturing their prisoners.
16 He was prevented □ coming because the roads were blocked.
17 She objected □ being treated like a child.
18 She is responsible □ arranging the meetings.
19 He insisted □ leaving punctually.
20 The children were not used □ having so much homework.

Übung 2

Infinitiv oder Gerundium? Achte auf die Bedeutungsunterschiede.

1 I remember □ (meet) him in London. It was a long time ago.
2 Always remember □ (say) 'thank you' when you receive a present.
3 Don't forget □ (lock) your car when you go into the house.
4 She regretted □ (give) him all her trust.
5 Can you remember □ (inform) me well in advance about your plans?
6 The mechanic tried □ (explain) the engine to him, but it was too complicated.
7 My uncle liked □ (play) chess.
8 He regrets □ (spend) money on useless things, but is always tempted to go on □ (do) so.
9 He stopped □ (go) to the cinema as he considered it a waste of time.
10 When they saw the accident, they stopped □ (help) the injured people.
11 I didn't mean □ (say) that I didn't like the idea.
12 On his way to the cabinet meeting the minister stopped □ (talk) to the reporters.
13 I'm very busy at the moment, but I'll try □ (phone) you later.
14 This disaster means □ (start) all over again.
15 After the manager had outlined his plan, he went on □ (explain) it in more detail.

Übung 3

Kombiniere die einzelnen Satzteile. Achte darauf, daß die Sätze Sinn ergeben.

1	The minister suggested . . .	A	speaking and returned to his seat.
2	The doctor advised him to give up . . .	B	meeting again next Wednesday.
3	He finished . . .	C	losing all your money.
4	When they heard the joke, they couldn't help . . .	D	smoking inside a garage.
5	Don't go to the casino, you risk . . .	E	laughing.
6	The official regulations do not permit . . .	F	drinking.
7	As a child John never went to the seaside because his parents disliked . . .	G	typing without looking at the keys.
8	If you want to be a good secretary you must practise . . .	H	living in the country.
9	Lack of information forced the reporters to delay . . .	I	spending their holidays in crowded places.
10	I hate life in the city; I miss . . .	J	publishing the document until Monday.

Übung 4

Setze die angegebenen Wörter in der richtigen Form ein.

wait · cry · meet · hear · get up · laugh · read · worry

1 It's no use ☐ over spilt milk.
2 When he had to go to school, he got used to ☐ early.
3 I like this book. It's really worth ☐ .
4 The train has left, so it's no use ☐ any longer.
5 His joke was so funny that she couldn't help ☐ .
6 Although they spoke very quietly, he couldn't help ☐ what they said.
7 How about ☐ me at 8 o'clock?
8 It's all over, so there's no point ☐ about the consequences.

Übung 5

Infinitiv oder Gerundium?

1 She enjoys ☐ (cook) for her old parents.
2 How about ☐ (go) abroad this summer?
3 We hope ☐ (meet) him soon.
4 The doctor tried ☐ (save) the patient's life.
5 The reporter said he would be interested in ☐ (interview) the minister.
6 He seemed to be very impolite, but he didn't mean ☐ (offend) anyone.
7 He suggested ☐ (meet) me outside the theatre.
8 He avoided ☐ (look) at his father.
9 He couldn't help ☐ (roar) with laughter.
10 John decided ☐ (see) the film about animals.

11 What does he expect me □ (do)?
12 The minister delayed □ (inform) the press because he was afraid of an outcry.
13 The driver stopped □ (drink) a cup of coffee and then went on.
14 The doctor didn't hesitate □ (tell) his patient to lose weight.
15 Don't forget □ (give) him the money you promised.
16 We can't afford □ (go) on holiday.
17 You've got enough money, so stop □ (worry) about it.
18 He meant □ (talk) to me about it, but forgot.
19 What about □ (spend) a weekend in London?
20 We are looking forward to □ (visit) you.

E Das Partizip

Ebenso wie der Infinitiv und das Gerundium ist das Partizip ein sprachliches Mittel, um sich knapp und klar auszudrücken.

Das Partizip steht:

- nach Verben der Ruhe und Bewegung wie **come, lie, remain, run, sit, stand, stay, walk.**

He sits reading until midnight every night.
I get annoyed when he stands there staring into space.

- in Verbindung mit dem Partizip Präsens bei zwei zur gleichen Zeit ablaufenden Handlungen.

He stands talking to friends while she runs around looking for work.

- anstelle eines Relativsatzes hinter dem Substantiv, zu dem es gehört.

The man sitting in the car explained what had happened.

- nach Verben der sinnlichen Wahrnehmung **(feel, find, hear, look, notice, observe, see, watch),** wenn der Ablauf einer Handlung betont werden soll. Sonst wird der Infinitiv verwendet, besonders bei Aufzählungen.

  I saw the dog swimming across the river.

  He saw him enter the room, open the window and sit down.

- nach den Verben **have** und **get** (lassen, veranlassen).

  He had the roof of his house repaired. *(Er ließ es machen.)*
  Aber: He had repaired the roof of his house before the storm. *(Er hat es selber gemacht.)*

Das Partizip steht anstelle eines Adverbialsatzes:

– der Zeit.	When he watches TV, he always eats chocolates.	When watching TV, he always eats chocolates.
	While he was writing a letter, he remembered he had to go to the bank.	While writing a letter, he remembered he had to go to the bank.
	After she had finished the letters, she went home.	After finishing/Having finished the letters, she went home.
– des Grundes.	As she had already seen the film, she didn't want to see it again.	Having already seen the film, she didn't want to see it again.
– der Art und Weise.	He sat there and cried for help.	He sat there crying for help.
– der Einräumung.	Although he was poor himself, he helped as much as he could.	(Al)Though being poor himself, he helped as much as he could.
– der Bedingung.	If she had been better informed, she would have come earlier.	If better informed, she would have come earlier.
– in festen Redewendungen.	considering (his age)	*wenn man (sein Alter) in Betracht zieht*
	generally speaking	*allgemein gesprochen*
	strictly speaking	*genau genommen*
	roughly speaking	*grob gerechnet*
	plainly speaking	*offen gesagt*
	talking of	*wenn man von . . . spricht*
	weather/time permitting	*wenn das Wetter/die Zeit es zuläßt*
	supposing you . . .	*angenommen, du/Sie . . .*

Übung 1

Ersetze den Adverbialsatz durch eine Partizipialkonstruktion.

Beispiel: While I was watching TV, I heard the telephone ring.
While watching TV, I heard the telephone ring.

1 As he was short of money, he couldn't afford the book he wanted to buy.
2 After he had seen the exhibition, he decided to order a new computer.
3 While she was preparing lunch, she heard a strange noise.
4 After I had realized it was so late, I ran faster and faster.
5 After he had changed his wet clothes, he sat down and enjoyed the evening paper.
6 After he had locked his vehicle, the driver went for lunch.
7 While we were sitting in the theatre, we suddenly noticed our neighbour in the second row.
8 When he realized the danger, he stopped immediately.
9 After they had sat on the beach for a few hours, they decided to go to a restaurant.
10 Although I tried my best to be on time, I didn't manage because of the traffic jams.

Übung 2

Verkürze die Sätze mit Hilfe einer Partizipialkonstruktion.

Beispiel: He closed all the windows and then left the house.
After closing all the windows, he left the house.
Having closed all the windows, he left the house.

She looked at the calendar and remembered it was her father's birthday.
Looking at the calendar, she remembered it was her father's birthday.

1 He put the screwdriver aside and left the garage.
2 He finished his tea and started work again.
3 She looked at her watch and realized it was time to leave.
4 He reached for the phone and rang the local hospital.
5 The mechanic repaired our car and then sent us a bill.
6 She looked into her purse and remembered she hadn't been to the bank.
7 She did the shopping and then went to a café for lunch.
8 He stood in the shower and sang a song.
9 He had missed the bus and had to wait for the next one.
10 The detective hoped to catch the thief and so he searched everywhere.
11 I knew he was looking for me, so I tried to avoid meeting him.
12 Peter was exhausted and lay down to have a rest.
13 He thought it would rain and so took an umbrella.
14 She hoped for good weather and so went to Italy.
15 He passed his medical exam and then opened his own practice.

"For every person wishing to teach, there are at least thirty not wanting to be taught."

Übung 3

Setze ein: Infinitiv oder Partizip.

1 I saw them ☐ (stand) at the corner ☐ (talk) to each other.
2 We heard the band ☐ (play) a nice march.
3 Mr Smith saw the burglar ☐ (break into) his neighbour's house and he quickly phoned the police.
4 We stood on the quay and watched the ship ☐ (disappear) into the distance.
5 I heard him ☐ (go) downstairs, ☐ (open) the door and ☐ (leave) the house.
6 Let's ring the bell again. I'm sure he's at home because I saw him ☐ (enter) the house a few minutes ago.
7 When I drove past the bus-stop, I saw him ☐ (wait) for the bus.
8 Did you notice anyone ☐ (watch) you on your way to our meeting place?
9 She looked out of the window and noticed an ambulance ☐ (stop) outside her house.
10 I heard you ☐ (play) the piano when I walked past your house yesterday.

6

Die indirekte Rede

Während in der direkten Rede der Sprecher/die Sprecherin zitiert wird, berichtet man in der indirekten Rede, was eine Person gesagt hat.
Bei der Umwandlung eines in der direkten Rede stehenden Satzes in einen in der indirekten findet eine Reihe von Veränderungen statt.

A Zeitverschiebung

Steht das einleitende Verb in der einfachen Gegenwart, im Perfekt oder in der Zukunft, ändert sich das Tempus der direkten Rede in der indirekten nicht. Das Wort **that** kann meist wegfallen.

Ohne Änderungen

Bob: "I like my English teacher."	Bob says (has said/will say) (that) he likes his English teacher.

Steht das einleitende Verb in der Vergangenheit, verändert sich das Tempus in der indirekten Rede.

Mit Änderungen

simple present "I like my English teacher."	**simple past** Bob said (that) he liked his English teacher.
present perfect "I have never seen such a wonderful picture."	**past perfect** Bob said (that) he had never seen such a wonderful picture.
simple past "I was ill for two weeks."	**past perfect** Bob said (that) he had been ill for two weeks.
will-future "I'll see Jane on Monday."	**would + infinitive** Bob said (that) he would see Jane on Monday.
going to-future "I'm going to London soon."	**was/were going to** Bob said (that) he was going to London soon.

Die Änderungen in der Verlaufsform entsprechen denen der jeweiligen Zeitverschiebungen der einfachen Formen in der indirekten Rede.	**progressive form** "I am (have been/was/will be) learning English."	Bob said he was (had been/had been/would be) learning English.

B Weitere Veränderungen

Bei den Adverbialbestimmungen treten folgende Veränderungen ein:

here	⋙→	there	ago	⋙→	before
now	⋙→	then	last week	⋙→	the previous week
today	⋙→	that day			
tomorrow	⋙→	the next day	next week	⋙→	the following week
yesterday	⋙→	the day before			

Pronomen und Possessivadjektive werden gewöhnlich von der ersten oder zweiten zur dritten Person verschoben.	Mary said, "I have forgotten the answer."	Mary said (that) she had forgotten the answer.

Mögliche Veränderungen:

Personalpronomen	I, you	*(Singular)*	⋙→ he, she
	we, you	*(Plural)*	⋙→ they
Possessivpronomen	my, your	*(Singular)*	⋙→ his, her
	our, your	*(Plural)*	⋙→ their

Eine Ausnahme sind die Fälle, in denen eine Person von sich selbst berichtet.	I said, "I like my book."	I told him (that) I liked my book.
Auf die gleiche Weise werden **this** und **these** zu **that** und **those**.	Mark said, "I'll take this pullover and these shirts."	Mark said (that) he would take that pullover and those shirts.
Fragesätze werden u.a. durch **ask, want to know** eingeleitet, und die Zeitverschiebungen entsprechen denen von Aussagesätzen in der indirekten Rede. Gibt es kein Fragewort, muß **if** oder **whether** verwendet werden.	"Do you like it?" John asked him.	John asked him whether/if he liked it.
Bei Bitten, Ratschlägen, Einladungen und Befehlssätzen stehen Verben wie **advised, asked, invited, ordered, told** mit dem Infinitiv + **to**.	Mr Jones to Bob: "Don't forget it." Lawyer: "Tell the police the truth, John."	Mr Jones told Bob not to forget it. The lawyer advised John to tell the police the truth.

Vorschläge werden mit **suggest** und dem Gerundium oder **that** + **should** + Infinitiv wiedergegeben.	John: "Let's leave earlier than planned."	John suggested leaving (that we should leave) earlier than planned.
Bei den Hilfsverben treten folgende Veränderungen ein:	can → could may → might must → had to	shall → should will → would
Aber: Keine Änderungen bei **would, could, might, should, ought to.**	Bob: "I could not do it for them." Doctor: "You ought to eat more, Jane."	Bob said (that) he could not do it for them. The doctor told Jane (that) she ought to eat more.

Übung 1

Wandle die folgenden Sätze in die indirekte Rede um und benutze **he/she said.**

1 "I saw him on Monday."
2 "I cannot work all day."
3 "You can come whenever you want to."
4 "I'll visit you in hospital."
5 "I hope to have my own car soon."
6 "She was jealous of his success."
7 "I've just bought a new washing machine."
8 "I've nothing to say."
9 "My son wants to become a lawyer."
10 "I'm living with my aunt in London."
11 "London is a very interesting place to visit."
12 "She is not at home – she has gone shopping."
13 "He's missed the bus because he got up too late."
14 "I hope to be home in time for the concert."
15 "Business has deteriorated, so a lot of young people have left town."
16 "There's been a terrible crash and the entrance to the airport is blocked."
17 "The new theatre season will open next week."
18 "I've no idea what to do with the broken car."
19 "She's an excellent student and has always worked hard."
20 "There were a lot of people at the football match."
21 "John has been in prison for ten years."
22 "The mountains proved too high for the group."
23 "I've got something to tell my son, but nobody is allowed to listen."
24 "I don't like his new coat at all."

"But, dear – I didn't tell your mother she was wrong. I only said that the dictionary didn't agree with her about something!"

Übung 2

Setze die folgenden Sätze in die indirekte Rede. Benutze die vorgegebenen Satzanfänge.

1 "I cannot get the car started because I have lost the key."
He pointed out . . .

2 "I cannot see through the glasses the doctor gave me."
He said . . .

3 "I may not be in time."
She remarked . . .

4 "Nothing I can do will help him."
The teacher complained . . .

5 "They can come whenever they want to."
My friend said . . .

6 "Our father can speak English fluently."
The children remarked . . .

7 "We shall never see him again."
We complained . . .

8 "I must do everything myself."
The school caretaker shouted . . .

9 "I will know the answer soon."
The reporter announced . . .

10 "Our mother will be eighty next Monday."
They pointed out . . .

11 "I cannot possibly come. It's far too late."
Joan said . . .

12 "I can get the books from the library in the afternoon if you want me to."
My sister pointed out . . .

13 "I cannot come at 8 o'clock because I must wash and dress my patient."
The nurse said . . .

14 "You can park your car in the garage."
The manager told Anne . . .

15 "I can give you the exact time of your next train."
The inspector told John . . .

16 "We will wait for Mary at the station."
My sisters said . . .

17 "The paint will soon be dry enough to walk on."
The painter mentioned . . .

18 "Tom, you must help me at all costs."
She insisted . . .

19 "I won't show you my picture until it is finished."
The artist told his friends . . .

20 "I have to go to an ear specialist because I cannot hear properly."
Henry told me . . .

Übung 3

Wandle die folgenden Sätze in die indirekte Rede um. Achte auf die Pronomen und adverbialen Bestimmungen.

1. "I'll meet you tomorrow."
   He said to Ann . . .
2. "Have you read these books?"
   He asked John . . .
3. "What happened last night?"
   He asked . . .
4. "Yesterday we went to a lovely concert."
   He mentioned to his parents-in-law . . .
5. "As it is extremely foggy today, we cannot leave the harbour now."
   The captain remarked . . .
6. "I cannot see you today, because I'm at work until 8 o'clock."
   He told her . . .
7. "I'm having a driving lesson this afternoon."
   He remembered . . .
8. "I remember that you had a different opinion five months ago."
   He said to Anne . . .
9. "I cannot think why he didn't want to see me last Monday."
   He remarked . . .
10. "Did you meet her yesterday when you were at the station?"
    He asked her . . .
11. "My brother isn't at home, he left a week ago."
    She answered . . .
12. "We're leaving for London tonight."
    He remarked on the phone . . .
13. "Did you go to the theatre last night?"
    She asked me . . .
14. "I read this novel a long time ago and still find it interesting."
    She said . . .
15. "Where were you last week?"
    His father asked John . . .
16. "How long have you been working here?"
    The new secretary asked her colleague . . .
17. "I always like to spend my holidays in this beautiful area."
    She pointed out . . .
18. "Why don't you come back tomorrow if you want to stay another day?"
    He asked her . . .
19. "The workers will go back to work tomorrow."
    The manager told the reporter . . .
20. "Where were you last night when the fire broke out in your house, Mr Jones?"
    The detective inquired . . .

Übung 4

Forme die direkten Fragesätze um. Benutze die vorgegebenen Satzanfänge.

1 "Have you seen him lately?"
He asked me . . .

2 "Do you prefer going by car or by bus?"
She asked me . . .

3 "What have you done with all the money I gave you?"
He asked his son . . .

4 "How did you escape from prison?"
The policeman asked the recaptured thief . . .

5 "How much is this beautiful car?"
The salesman was asked . . .

6 "Where can I change my money?"
He asked the bank clerk . . .

7 "Is that all you have to say?"
The ticket inspector asked the passenger . . .

8 "What have you done to deserve such punishment?"
They were asked . . .

9 "When did you decide to leave the country?"
The judge asked the accused man . . .

10 "Why won't you allow me to see my husband in prison?"
The woman asked the warden . . .

11 "When will I see you again?"
He asked his girl-friend . . .

12 "Have you bought a new TV set yet?"
He asked me . . .

13 "Can you tell us what time he was murdered?"
The police asked the doctor . . .

14 "Would you like to see my son's latest letter from Italy?"
He asked her . . .

15 "Has he told you that he won't be able to come to your party?"
She asked me . . .

16 "Can you ask your former headmaster for a letter of recommendation?"
My friend wanted to know . . .

17 "Did you enjoy your holiday in Australia?"
Our neighbour asked us . . .

18 "How long have you been suffering from this terrible cold?"
The doctor asked me . . .

19 "When does the next train for Manchester leave?"
I inquired . . .

20 "Why don't you ever listen to what I'm saying?"
Mrs Smith asked her daughter . . .

21 "Are you enjoying your lunch, Mr Smith?"
She wanted to know . . .

22 "Is the water clean enough to go swimming here?"
The children inquired . . .

"Yes, of course my wife said she was expecting you to have dinner with us. We argued about it for half an hour this morning."

23 "Is your car always broken?"
He asked me ironically . . .
24 "What's wrong with it?"
She asked . . .
25 "Can you hear the thunder in the distance?"
John asked his father . . .

Übung 5

Wandle die Befehlssätze um. Benutze die vorgegebenen Satzanfänge.

1 "Take these flowers to Aunt Margaret, Jane."
Her mother told . . .
2 "Keep the doors closed."
The teacher ordered the children . . .
3 "Don't drive so fast."
The driving instructor warned the learner . . .
4 "Don't write more than 400 words."
The teacher reminded the pupils . . .
5 "Take five pills a day."
The doctor advised the patient . . .
6 "Try harder this time."
The examiner told the candidate . . .
7 "Don't forget your money this time."
He warned his friend . . .
8 "Get out of my room, Susan."
She told Susan . . .
9 "Pay at the exit, please."
The customers were asked . . .
10 "Write to me whenever you find time."
She told her sister . . .
11 "Don't waste your time."
He warned his son . . .
12 "Be careful when driving on the other side of the road in Great Britain."
He told us . . .
13 "Don't hang around – get moving."
The teacher ordered his pupils . . .
14 "Don't forget to say 'thank you' for all the Christmas presents you had."
The mother reminded her little son . . .
15 "Don't touch the switch. You may cause an explosion."
He advised us . . .
16 "Give it a try and see if it works."
Anne told John . . .
17 "Do what I tell you."
He ordered the boys . . .
18 "Put the spare parts here."
The mechanic told his assistant . . .
19 "Take a week's rest."
The doctor advised his patient . . .
20 "Start the attack at 5 o'clock."
The officer ordered his men . . .

7 Bedingungssätze

Bedingungssätze bestehen aus dem **if**-Satz und dem Hauptsatz.
In ihnen werden die Bedingungen oder Voraussetzungen genannt, unter denen etwas geschehen soll.
Man unterscheidet drei Haupttypen, die immer wieder zu Verwechslungen führen.

Typ 1

Hier ist die Bedingung leicht zu erfüllen, und die Handlung im Hauptsatz wird aller Wahrscheinlichkeit nach eintreten.

if-Satz	**Hauptsatz**
Gegenwart	**will-future (can, may** usw.**)** + *Infinitiv*
If he reads it,	he will know the answer.

Hier steht in beiden Sätzen die Gegenwart, weil eine klare Verbindung zwischen Neben- und Hauptsatz besteht. **If** hat hier die Bedeutung von **whenever**.

If it rains, the ground gets wet.

Typ 2

Die Bedingung ist weniger leicht zu erfüllen, und die Wahrscheinlichkeit, daß die im Hauptsatz zum Ausdruck gebrachte Handlung eintreten wird, ist wenig wahrscheinlich.

if-Satz	**Hauptsatz**
Vergangenheit	**would (could, might)** + *Infinitiv* could = Fähigkeit, might = Möglichkeit
If he read it,	he would know the answer.

Typ 3

Die Bedingung ist überhaupt nicht erfüllbar, weil die Handlung im **if**-Satz nicht stattgefunden hat.

if-Satz	**Hauptsatz**
Plusquamperfekt	**would (could, might)** + *Partizip Perfekt*
If he had read it,	he would have known the answer.

Übung 1

Typ 1 Vervollständige die Sätze.

1 If I ☐ (meet) him, I ☐ (give) him the book he wants.
2 She ☐ (be) surprised if she ☐ (see) him earlier than she expects to.
3 If she ☐ (not be) there on time, I ☐ (begin) without her.
4 I ☐ (lend) you some money if you ☐ (promise) to give it back soon.
5 If you ☐ (go on) telling lies, I ☐ (be) angry with you.
6 The police ☐ (let) you know if they ☐ (find) your stolen car.
7 If you ☐ (not switch) on your headlights, you ☐ (endanger) your life.
8 If he ☐ (want) to be more successful, he ☐ (have to) work harder.
9 If she ☐ (go on) drinking like that, she ☐ (ruin) her health in no time.
10 If you ☐ (want) to read this book, I ☐ (get) a copy from the library.
11 If you ☐ (drop) the vase, it ☐ (break) immediately.
12 I am sure he ☐ (believe) the story if you ☐ (tell) him everything.
13 If we ☐ (not get) any oil, we ☐ (freeze) next winter.
14 If you ☐ (like), I ☐ (help) you whenever you want me to.
15 We ☐ (come) over to your house if you ☐ (give) us a call.

Übung 2

Typ 2 Vervollständige die Sätze.

1 If I ☐ (have) a car, I ☐ (go) myself.
2 I ☐ (help) him if I ☐ (be) you.
3 I ☐ (buy) the television set if I ☐ (have) the chance.
4 If we ☐ (win) in the lottery, we ☐ (buy) a mansion in the country.
5 If I ☐ (give) him some money, he ☐ (only, spend) it on alcohol and cigarettes.
6 If you ☐ (work) harder, you ☐ (be) successful in your exams.
7 I ☐ (avoid) this town if I ☐ (be) you.
8 If he ☐ (have) the money, he ☐ (not hesitate) to support the refugees.
9 They ☐ (visit) them if they ☐ (have) their address in Manchester.
10 If you ☐ (stop) drinking, you ☐ (save) a lot of money.
11 He ☐ (be) surprised if he ☐ (see) you under these circumstances.
12 If we ☐ (have) a better bus system, people ☐ (get) around faster in our town.
13 Old people ☐ (be) better off if their pensions ☐ (be) higher.
14 If I ☐ (be) responsible for education, I ☐ (spend) more money on books and classroom equipment.
15 If I ☐ (borrow) your watch, I ☐ (not have to) buy a new one.
16 He ☐ (learn) more German if he ☐ (not speak) so much English.

17 If he □ (take) more exercise, he □ (always, not feel) so tired.
18 If you □ (clean) your shoes, your mother □ (not be) so angry.
19 The two boys □ (not have to) walk so far if they □ (live) nearer the school.
20 If the restaurant □ (be) open, we □ (be able to) have a lovely meal.

Übung 3

Typ 3 Vervollständige die Sätze.

1 If you □ (work) harder, you □ (pass) your exams.
2 If the police □ (not notice) the gang, they □ (rob) the bank.
3 The coach driver □ (reach) London earlier if he □ (take) the motorway.
4 I □ (not lend) him my car if I □ (know) how unreliable he is.
5 If we □ (have) more time, we □ (see) The Tower.
6 My friend □ (not miss) his bus if he □ (leave) home earlier.
7 The station □ (not burn down) if the people □ (notice) the fire sooner.
8 She □ (not walk) if she □ (realize) how dirty the country road was.
9 If I □ (understand) your story right from the beginning, I □ (not ask) so many questions.
10 The housewife □ (buy) more fruit and vegetables if she □ (know) how expensive everything was going to be the next day.
11 You □ (not have) a breakdown if you □ (repair) your car.
12 If I □ (know) the time of your arrival, I □ (pick) you up at the station.
13 The painter □ (receive) a lot of money for that painting if he □ (not sell) it years ago.
14 We □ (go) on that trip if it □ (not start) to pour with rain.
15 We □ (go) to the concert if we □ (get) tickets, but they were sold out.
16 If he □ (not be interrupted) so often, he □ (repair) the televison set more quickly.
17 I □ (tell) you if I □ (know) earlier.
18 If he □ (wear) a tie, the doorkeeper □ (allow) him to enter the club.
19 Many people □ (not lose) their lives if the lifeboats □ (be) in order.
20 We □ (reach) the airport in time if the taxi □ (not break down).

Übung 4

Typ 1–3 Kombiniere die entsprechenden Satzhälften. Achte darauf, daß sie Sinn ergeben.

1 If you pass your exams . . .
2 You will break the glass . . .
3 You would feel better . . .
4 If we leave before 10 o'clock . . .
5 If I had known how miserable you were . . .
6 If you don't take off your wet clothes at once . . .
7 If the storm gets worse . . .
8 If I had a car . . .

A I would have visited you in hospital earlier.
B if you did more physical exercise.
C if you don't handle it with care.
D you will catch a cold.
E we will have a big party to celebrate.
F I would pick you up.
G we will get there in time.
H we won't be able to leave the harbour.

Übung 5

Typ 1–3 Kombiniere die entsprechenden Satzhälften. Achte darauf, daß sie Sinn ergeben.

1 If he was in . . .
2 If I lived in the city . . .
3 The milk will turn sour . . .
4 Your clothes will soon be dry . . .
5 He would have had to leave school . . .
6 If the police had taken a photograph of the criminal . . .
7 They would believe you . . .
8 If he admits his guilt now . . .
9 If you had had a seat nearer the stage . . .
10 If I see him tonight . . .

A they will give him another chance.
B he would answer the door.
C if you leave them out in the sun.
D if you told them how it really happened.
E if the headmaster had found out.
F you would have seen everything much better.
G they would have recognized him.
H I would move to the country-side at once.
I I'll remind him of the meeting tomorrow afternoon.
J if you don't put it in the fridge.

"We do not have toothbrushes with motor-oil, sir. Perhaps it would be better if you ordered your lunch in English . . ."

8

Präpositionen

Es gibt Präpositionen des Ortes oder der Richtung. Die meisten stehen auch für Zeitangaben oder werden im übertragenen Sinne gebraucht.
Die folgende Tabelle verzeichnet die wichtigsten Präpositionen und ihre Verwendung. Das sind nur einige Beispiele für den Gebrauch der Präpositionen. Besonders im übertragenen Sinne gibt es noch viele weitere Möglichkeiten.

	räumlich	**zeitlich**	**übertragen**
about (um herum, gegen)	They walked about the town.	They arrived about midnight.	She forgot all about it.
after (nach)	Your name is after mine on the list.	They left after two hours.	Judy was named after her aunt.
among (unter, zwischen)	The passport was among my books.		There was a disagreement among the politicians.
at (in, an, bei, gegen, um, zu)	He waited at the station/at the door/ at home. Who threw the stone at the window?	I saw him at Easter/ at 5 o'clock/at that moment/at night.	He smiled at her. She was good at French. She was hard at work.
before (vor)	F comes before G in the alphabet.	We arrived before the evening meal.	He was brought before the judge.
behind (hinter)	Who sits behind her?	The bus was behind schedule.	She went to New York and left her children behind.
beside (neben)	Sit beside me.		This is beside the point.
besides (außer)			There were three people besides me.

	räumlich	zeitlich	übertragen
between (zwischen, unter)	She sat between her parents.	It was between five and six o'clock.	It's an agreement between us.
by (bei, bis, von, dadurch, mit usw.)	We walked down a lane by the river.	He travelled by day. I'll finish by tomorrow. I pay by the month.	He came by bus. The novel was by Hemingway. She won by cheating.
for (für, seit, aus)	I walked for miles.	He was imprisoned for life. She has been learning English for four years.	I did it for fun.
from (aus, von)	He comes from Paris.	He worked from 6 o'clock to 8 o'clock.	I know that from my own experience.
in (in, auf, an, bei)	She lives in London.	I did it in 3 hours.	Give me the word in English, please.
of (von, an, nach usw.)	It is north of London.	Within a month of her death.	She died of cancer.
on (auf, an, zu, in usw.)	It is on the table.	It was on Friday.	The house is on fire.
over (über)	He walked over the bridge.	Over the next few days . . .	There were over three hundred books.
since (seit)		He has been in London since 1945.	
to (zu, in, bis)	Go to London.	It is ten to five.	They danced to the music.
up (hinauf)	He went up the ladder.		He made up a good story.
with (bei, mit)	He lives with his sister.		The gangster killed him with a knife.

Folgende Präpositionen verdienen besondere Beachtung, da sie sehr fehlerträchtig sind.

at – in

at „an einem bestimmten Punkt" (Festtage, Häuser, Stationen).	at Easter at Buckingham Palace at Piccadilly *Aber:* on Christmas Day/Easter Sunday

in
zeigt den Zeitpunkt an, an dem etwas geschehen wird.

in three months' time
in the evening
Aber: at night

bei Städten, Provinzen, Regionen.

in London

for – since

for (seit)
zeigt den Zeitraum an, in dem etwas geschieht. Häufig im Perfekt.

He has lived here for five years.

since (seit)
zeigt den Zeitpunkt an, an dem etwas geschieht. Häufig im Perfekt.

He has lived here since 1980.

by – with

by
wird verwendet bei Transportmitteln oder zur Angabe eines Mediums.

by car
by airmail
driven by electricity

with
bezieht sich auf ein Instrument oder Werkzeug.

with a knife/hammer

between – among

between (zwischen)
wird gebraucht, wenn es sich um zwei Personen/Dinge handelt.

He stood between his mother and his father.

among (zwischen)
wird verwendet, wenn es sich um mehr als zwei Personen/Dinge handelt.

The students at the party talked among themselves.

behind – after

behind (hinter, nach)
Gegensatz: **in front of**

He walked behind me. *(d.h. nicht vor mir)*

after (hinter ... her)

The police ran after the thief. *(d.h. um ihn zu fangen)*

Übung 1

Entscheide: **at** oder **in**.

1 ☐ the age of five
2 ☐ good time
3 ☐ 6.30 pm
4 ☐ the end of this year
5 ☐ a few weeks
6 ☐ midnight
7 ☐ lunchtime
8 ☐ any moment
9 ☐ twenty minutes
10 ☐ five years' time
11 ☐ daybreak
12 ☐ a short time
13 ☐ January
14 ☐ the weekend
15 ☐ 1992

Übung 2

Entscheide: **at** oder **in**.

1 He was standing ☐ a long queue inside the post office.
2 We have to stop ☐ the traffic lights when they are red.
3 We always spend our holidays ☐ England.
4 ☐ Easter Christians celebrate the resurrection of Christ.
5 He works ☐ London.
6 There is a hotel ☐ the end of this street.
7 You have to turn right ☐ the next crossroads.
8 My parents have lived ☐ this town for twenty years now.
9 We met him ☐ a party.
10 He asked me to wait for him ☐ the bus stop.
11 The Empire State Building is one of the highest buildings ☐ the world.
12 We like swimming ☐ the sea.
13 There was a 'No Smoking' sign ☐ the entrance of the cinema.
14 He is very good ☐ French.
15 He often works in the garden ☐ the evening.

Übung 3

Setze ein: **since** oder **for**.

1 He has not seen his friend ☐ last year.
2 She has never been back to her old school ☐ she left it.
3 The couple have been married ☐ ten years.
4 They have been away ☐ six months now.
5 I have known him ☐ our childhood days.
6 I have not talked to him ☐ a long time.
7 This is the most interesting book I've read ☐ years.
8 I have been waiting for you ☐ half an hour.
9 My friend has been in hospital ☐ last October.
10 I have had a terrible headache ☐ yesterday.
11 The windows are dirty. Nobody has cleaned them ☐ weeks.
12 The police are looking for the little boy who has not been seen ☐ last Tuesday.
13 I have not played tennis ☐ last summer.
14 It is very dry because it hasn't rained ☐ three months.
15 I have been working here ☐ 1983.

Übung 4

Entscheide zwischen **by** und **with**.

1. He helped me ☐ my homework.
2. They left the house ☐ their parents.
3. The team arrived ☐ train.
4. They travelled to London ☐ bus.
5. It's better to send this ☐ post.
6. He gave me a hand ☐ the ladder as it was so heavy.
7. My mother removed the stain ☐ soap.
8. The table was covered ☐ newspapers.
9. He paid ☐ cheque.
10. It was so dark that we had to read ☐ candlelight.
11. What do you mean ☐ that?
12. This product is still made ☐ hand.

Übung 5

Setze ein: **among** oder **between**.

1. I cannot see any difference ☐ these two pictures.
2. He has been living ☐ the natives for more than ten years now.
3. She's sitting ☐ her sister and her mother.
4. He divided the sweets ☐ the five boys.
5. All the pears he gave us were bad. There wasn't a good one ☐ them.
6. The small house stood ☐ the two tall buildings.
7. The neighbours have always quarrelled ☐ themselves.
8. The twins look so alike. I cannot distinguish ☐ them.
9. There was a spy ☐ the members of staff.
10. Call me ☐ ten and eleven in the morning.

Übung 6

Entscheide zwischen **after** und **behind**.

1. The police ran ☐ the gangster.
2. The dog chased ☐ the cat.
3. The hotel was ☐ the restaurant.
4. The spies met ☐ closed doors.
5. They went for a long walk ☐ their meal.
6. There was a garden ☐ the house.
7. The train is always ☐ schedule.
8. He is very ☐ the times.
9. I'll see you ☐ breakfast.
10. He talked a lot about his friend ☐ his back.

Übung 7

Setze die fehlenden Präpositionen ein.

1 I will arrive □ exactly seven o'clock.
2 It will happen □ 10 minutes.
3 He has lived here □ 1956.
4 I always stay □ my aunt when I'm in England.
5 He had to choose □ two possibilities.
6 She isn't very good □ Spanish.
7 We have not had any rain □ weeks.
8 She always goes to see her grandfather □ Mondays.
9 I have not seen him □ he was ten.
10 I found his letter □ all the books on my desk.
11 How do you say this □ English?
12 She is very busy □ the moment.
13 He should arrive □ a short time.
14 He has been suffering from terrible pain □ a long time.
15 Have you lived in this house □ you were born?
16 They will be away □ Monday till Sunday.
17 □ those days we used to see him regularly.
18 She died □ the age of ninety-two.
19 We often go for walks □ the afternoon.
20 He will be twenty □ January 2nd.

"It's just like being at home, isn't it, Bert?"

9

Aussprache

Die richtige *Aussprache* ist beim Erlernen der englischen Sprache von entscheidender Bedeutung. Nur durch ständiges Üben kann sie gefestigt und für den täglichen Gebrauch verfügbar gemacht werden.

In den folgenden Abschnitten wird versucht, besonders diejenigen Laute zu berücksichtigen, die fortgeschrittenen Lernenden, für die dieses Buch bestimmt ist, immer noch Schwierigkeiten machen. Die phonetischen Symbole entsprechen denen der 14. Auflage des **Everyman's English Pronouncing Dictionary** von D. Jones und A.C. Gimson (London 1988).

Vokale

iː	cl**ea**n	ɪ	m**i**st
ɑː	d**ar**k	ʌ	c**u**t
ɔː	l**aw**	ɒ	p**o**t
uː	m**oo**n	ʊ	p**u**t
ɜː	b**ir**d		
e	p**e**n		
ə	**a**bout		
æ	man		

Diphthonge

eɪ	m**ai**n
aɪ	s**i**gn
ɔɪ	b**oy**
əʊ	th**ough**
aʊ	n**ow**
ɪə	b**eer**
eə	b**ear**
ʊə	p**oor**
ɔə	p**our**

Konsonanten

p	**p**ost	b	**b**ird	h	**h**im
t	**t**ea	d	**d**o	m	**m**an
k	**c**lean	g	**g**irl	n	so**n**
tʃ	**ch**ip	dʒ	**G**erman	ŋ	si**ng**
f	**f**un	v	**v**ice	l	**l**ight
θ	**th**in	ð	**th**em	r	**r**ight
s	**s**ign	z	**z**one	w	**w**ine
ʃ	**sh**ip	ʒ	mea**s**ure	j	**y**es

A Die einzelnen Vokale

1 Der Buchstabe 'a' und seine verschiedenen Aussprachemöglichkeiten

[æ]	gas, hat	[ɒ]	swamp, wallet	[eɪ]	ancient, radio	[e]	any, ate
[ɑː]	branch, chance	[ɔː]	all, war	[ə]	canoe, mustard		

Übung 1

Achte auf den 'odd man out'.

1 car, man, bang, barren, jazz
2 cabin, gravel, famous, pan, camel
3 all, always, clan, salt, Malta
4 what, watch, wash, gate, quality
5 base, waste, taste, chance, paste
6 law, reward, walk, quantity, straw

Übung 2

Lies laut und unterscheide zwischen [eɪ] und [æ].

able, case, chap, Cambridge, grave, labour, can, pan, ant, clan

Lies laut und unterscheide zwischen [ɑː] und [æ].

after, glass, sack, ban, father, master, bag, fathom, lack, disaster

Übung 3

Ordne das Wort dem entsprechenden phonetischen Symbol zu und markiere es mit einem +.

	ɒ	ɔː	æ	ɑː	eɪ	ə	e
ask							
t**a**ke							
all							
m**a**n							
sw**a**n							
b**a**ll							
s**a**lt							
l**a**bour							
h**a**ppy							
w**a**nt							
c**a**n't							
above							
ache							
about							
m**a**ny							

Übung 4

Lies laut und unterscheide zwischen [ɒ] [ɔː] [ɑː] und [eɪ].

cauliflower, laugh, launch, slaughter, applaud, sausage, pause, gauge, fault, laughter, Laurence, aunt, laundry, saucer, exhaust

2 Der Buchstabe 'e' und seine verschiedenen Aussprachemöglichkeiten

[iː]	fever, heel	[ɜː]	concern, search	[ɪ]	Greenwich, pretty	[uː]	crew, few
[e]	never, pen	[ɑː]	clerk, Hertford	[aɪ]	(n)either	[əʊ]	Beaujolais, sewing
[eɪ]	break, precis	[ɪə]	query, real	[eə]	bear, swear		

Übung 5

Achte auf den 'odd man out'.

1 appeal, increase, near, disease, repeat
2 earth, ear, early, earn, pearl
3 head, meaning, bread, dead, Reading
4 meat, decreasing, wealth, clean, bean
5 red, blemish, cedar, every, else
6 Edith, clever, ever, men, pen
7 medium, evening, lever, level, illegal

Übung 6

Achte auf die hervorgehobenen Buchstaben und ordne die Wörter den entsprechenden phonetischen Symbolen zu.

ch**ee**se, b**ea**rd, d**e**nse
ch**e**rry, d**ee**r, f**ea**st
either, h**ea**rt, br**ea**k
br**ea**th, h**ea**rd, n**ei**ther
pr**e**tty, s**e**w, bl**e**w, b**ea**r

iː	uː	ɪə	e
aɪ	eɪ	eə	ɪ
ɜː	əʊ	ɑː	

Übung 7

Lies laut und unterscheide:

[e] oder [iː] lemon, legal, help, demon, dentist, decency
[eə] oder [ɪə] beard, near, pear, clear, bear, hear, wear, weary
[iː] oder [e] seal, health, meal, peace, peach, death, pea

Übung 8

Achte auf den 'odd man out'.

1 several, zero, mend, ten, centre
2 bear, heart, tear, pear, swear
3 search, earth, heard, hearth, learned
4 deer, career, beer, sneeze, peer

3 Der Buchstabe 'i' und seine verschiedenen Aussprachemöglichkeiten

[aɪ] lie, pint [ɪ] pick, thick [iː] niece, police [ɜː] bird, shirt

Übung 9

Wie werden die folgenden Wörter ausgesprochen: [aɪ], [ɪ], [iː] oder [ɜː]?

rival, pin, sir, pie, bridge, whirl, fir, silent, die, sick, skirt, middle, machine, thirty, suite, magazine, police, bill, girl, figure, unique, still, stir, liberal, decide, fiction, Shirley, like, nice, thin, wipe, fine

Übung 10

Ordne das Wort dem entsprechenden phonetischen Symbol zu und markiere es mit einem +.

	ɪ	aɪ	iː	ɜː
p**i**ll				
p**i**lot				
t**i**ght				
t**i**me				
c**i**rcus				
c**i**nema				
mach**i**nery				

Übung 11

Wie werden die folgenden Wörter ausgesprochen: [ɪ], [iː] oder [ɜː]?

shirt, mirror, yield, piece, birth, siege, mischief, priest, finish, kindred, fatigue, sir, thick, idiom, vinegar, thirst, technique, linen, chimney, misty

4 Der Buchstabe 'o' und seine verschiedenen Aussprachemöglichkeiten

[ɒ] bother, hot
[ʌ] come, mother
[əʊ] comb, goal
[aʊ] crowd, now
[ʊ] wolf, woman
[uː] do, lose
[ɔː] order, organ

Übung 12

Ordne das Wort dem entsprechenden phonetischen Symbol zu und markiere es mit einem +.

	ɒ	ʌ	aʊ	ʊ	əʊ	uː	ɔː
b**o**x							
t**o**n							
c**o**llege							
fl**oo**d							
m**oo**n							
c**o**ach							
m**o**an							
owing							
t**o**wer							
w**o**man							
ought							

Übung 13

Achte auf den 'odd man out'.

1 bottle, cottage, copy, colour, gone
2 afternoon, hook, soothing, boots, loose
3 moral, product, voluntary, honour, no
4 son, one, onion, oven, dog

Übung 14

Vervollständige die Wörter mit den angegebenen Buchstaben.

1 c□mfortable
2 c□mment
3 t□ch
4 t□l
5 t□gh
6 cl□ck
7 w□nd
8 arr□
9 n□rish
10 sh□
11 h□d
12 sh□er

o **ou**
ow **oo**
oe

Übung 15

Lies die folgenden Wörter und unterscheide:

[əʊ] oder [ɔː] road, hoarse, board, loan, coarse, load, oar, coal, soar, boat
[ʌ] oder [əʊ] rough, shoulder, southern, tough, soul, country, boulder, courage, cousin, touch
[aʊ] oder [əʊ] allow, throw, show, blow, cow, now, snow, flow, how, fowl
[uː] oder [ʊ] fool, book, cook, proof, balloon, boot, shook, stood, mood, look

5 Der Buchstabe 'u' und seine verschiedenen Aussprachemöglichkeiten

[ʊ] butcher, pull	[uː] juice, pupil	[ə] figure, nature	[ʊə] during, sure
[ʌ] club, dull	[ɜː] curse, purse	[ɪ] business, busy	[e] burial, bury

Übung 16

Lies laut und unterscheide:

[ʊ] oder [ʌ] bullet, nut, full, sudden, bull, bush, struggle, cushion, study, but, stuff, punish, fun

[ʊ] oder [uː] music, pupil, butcher, use, pull, push, union, sugar, duke, ruin

[uː] oder [ʌ] tube, rum, tunnel, rumour, cunning, rude, culture, human gun, June

Übung 17

Achte auf die fettgedruckten Buchstaben und ordne die Wörter den richtigen phonetischen Symbolen zu.

n**u**ll, b**u**sy, m**u**scle, c**u**re
b**u**ilding, b**u**lb, b**u**rn, sec**u**rity
b**u**rial, tr**u**th, b**u**sh, diffic**u**lt
t**u**ne, t**u**mult, p**u**dding, ind**u**stry
p**u**lpit, p**u**rr, p**u**rpose, b**u**siness

ʊ	uː	ʊə	e
ɪ	ə	ɜː	ʌ

Übung 18

Achte auf den 'odd man out'.

1 button, cup, cut, fume, pun
2 dusk, public, gum, curb, number
3 vulnerable, during, muster, nun, dust
4 supper, sun, stunt, cuckoo, vulgar
5 culprit, tulip, dung, gulf, grumble

B Die einzelnen Konsonanten

Die Übungen zu den Konsonanten beschränken sich auf diejenigen, deren richtige Aussprache immer wieder Schwierigkeiten bereitet. Es handelt sich dabei hauptsächlich um das stimmlose und stimmhafte **s** [s, z] und das stimmlose und stimmhafte **th** [θ, ð].

1 Der Konsonant 's'

Anlautendes **s** ist stets stimmlos (**sign** [saɪn], **soul** [səʊl]) Auslautendes **s** ist nach stimmhaften Konsonanten stimmhaft (**boards** [bɔːdz]), nach stimmlosen Konsonanten stimmlos (**stops** [stɒps]); nach einem Zischlaut wird auslautendes **s** silbisch gesprochen (**dresses** ['dresɪz]).

Übung 1

[s], [z] und [ɪz] im Auslaut. Achte auf den 'odd man out'.

1 brings, resists, hears, gives, swims
2 cars, results, bears, birds, treasures
3 defeats, breaks, puts, tells, writes
4 oranges, books, desks, goats, barks
5 calls, pens, sees, exercises, rings
6 keeps, amounts, believes, looks, shouts
7 cleans, runs, follows, drives, walks
8 goes, does, speaks, shows, minds

Übung 2

Lies laut und unterscheide, ob [s], [z] oder [ɪz] im Auslaut.

opens, sings, looks, works, sleeps, kisses, lands, says, corrects, boxes, meets, rains, takes, drinks, wants, cages, defends, understands, becomes, makes, rules, matches, suits, decides, thinks, solves, reclines, constructs, doses, hiss, his

Übung 3

Entscheide, ob [s], [z] oder [ɪz] im Auslaut.

fights, dresses, crosses, marks, jumps, masses, eats, enters, gases, lights, buses, oranges, gets, goats, sticks, garages, backs, lettuces, lots, gazes, exercises, laces, hopes, houses, books

Übung 4

Achte auf das **s** am Ende jedes Wortes und entscheide, ob es [s], [z] oder [ɪz] ausgesprochen wird.

scenes, ceases, purchases, breathes, issues, sounds, aches, rounds, noises, ends, replies, succeeds, convinces, cigarettes, cigars, brackets, mistakes, heals, kills, needs, remembers, documents, balls, addresses, daughters, fastens, leases, sweets, presidents, parts, questions, races, loses, costs, sandwiches, banks, battles, presents, benches, crickets

Übung 5

Lies laut und entscheide, ob [z] oder [ɪz] im Auslaut.

transfers, figures, mattresses, flies, measures, boxes, mothers, messages, reads, fathers, wanders, knobs, wins, brothers, wonders, pieces, chases, produces, husbands, sausages, seems

Ein im Inlaut stehendes **s** ist in seiner Aussprache kaum regelhaft zu erfassen: **result** [rɪ'zʌlt], aber **generosity** [dʒenə'rɒsətɪ]. Auf jeden Fall ist die Benutzung eines Lexikons zu empfehlen, um die jeweils richtige Aussprache kontrollieren zu können.

Übung 6

Lies laut und unterscheide bei den hervorgehobenen **s** zwischen [s] oder [z].

1 whi**s**tle, clo**s**ely, ba**s**in, loo**s**ely, lo**s**ing, Tue**s**day, re**s**ist, increa**s**ing, hu**s**band, nece**ss**ary
2 de**s**olate, de**s**erve, hand**s**ome, de**s**ign, cha**s**ing, de**s**cent, clo**s**ing, era**s**er, jealou**s**y, ba**s**ement
3 de**s**ire, po**ss**ess, philo**s**ophy, ver**s**es, di**s**aster, per**s**on, lou**s**y, epi**s**ode, di**s**ea**s**e, decrea**s**ing
4 de**ss**ert, po**ss**ible, despi**s**e, noi**s**y, po**s**ing, bu**s**y, analy**sis**, lea**s**ing, ga**s**oline, choo**s**ing
5 rea**s**on, mi**ss**ile, Wedne**s**day, de**s**ecrate, re**s**ent, re**s**ource, per**s**onal, no**s**ey, mu**s**ic, kin**s**men

2 Der Konsonant 'th'

th im Anlaut: **them** [ðem], aber **thick** [θɪk].
Inlautendes **th** ist in Wörtern germanischer Herkunft stimmhaft (**father** ['fɑːðə]); in Wörtern lateinisch-griechischer Herkunft stimmlos (**author** ['ɔːθə]).
th vor stummem **e** gilt als inlautend und stimmhaft (**breathe** [briːð]).
Auslautendes **th** ist meist stimmlos (**month** [mʌnθ]).

Übung 7

Lies laut und unterscheide zwischen [ð] oder [θ].

them, thick, thing, theirs, thin, these, thus, though, think, throne there, thaw, thankful, therefore, thief, thimble, third, that, thirty, those, thought, thirsty, then, thousand, they

Übung 8

Achte auf den 'odd man out'.

1 breathe, wealth, path, worth, north
2 bathe, Smith, birth, beneath, wreath
3 tooth, moth, myth, smooth, wrath

10 Rechtschreibung und Interpunktion

Die englische Rechtschreibung ist oft als Schlechtschreibung bezeichnet worden. G.B. Shaw schlug einmal vor, das englische Wort **fish** [fɪʃ] als "ghoti" zu schreiben: **gh** wie in **enough**, das **o** wie in **women** und das **ti** wie in dem Wort **nation**. Dieser Unterschied ergibt sich aus der fehlenden einheitlichen Beziehung zwischen Laut und Schrift im Englischen. Ursache dafür ist, daß die heutige Orthographie auf das 15. Jahrhundert zurückgeht und nicht den im Laufe der Zeit eingetretenen Veränderungen in der Aussprache angepaßt worden ist.
Die folgende Aufstellung mag einen kleinen Eindruck vermitteln.

A Die Vokale

[ɑː]	part, pass, heart, clerk, aunt, calm
[iː]	machine, tree, leaf, piece, seize, key
[ɪ]	sit, city, pretty, countries, village
[e]	set, head, many, leopard
[ʌ]	sun, son, young, blood, does

Übung 1

Setze die angegebenen Vokale/Diphthonge in die entsprechenden Lücken ein.

a · e · ea · ee · ie · i · o

1 He is taller th□n his brother.
2 Th□n he went to London.
3 He wiped the sw□t from his eyes.
4 The little boy liked sw□ts most of all.
5 B□rs have almost died out.
6 I like English b□r. It tastes lovely.
7 His sp□ch was far too long.
8 He sp□ks English fluently.
9 It became very qu□t when he began to talk.
10 It was qu□te dark when he came home.
11 The advertising campaign had no □ffect on the sales of the company.
12 This decision will □ffect the future of the factory.

Übung 2

Setze die phonetischen Symbole in die entsprechenden orthographischen Zeichen um.

1 The blackb[ɔ:]d was full of drawings.
2 Something like that can happen in the c[ɔ:]se of events.
3 Here is a present f[ɔ:]r you.
4 The r[eɪ]n fell all day.
5 They called in v[eɪ]n for help.
6 Everybody has two [ɑ:]ms.
7 A vulture is a bird of pr[eɪ].
8 Can I [ɔ:]lter the time of our meeting?
9 A v[eɪ]n is a tube in the body which carries blood to the heart.
10 The shoes are made of c[ɔ:]se material.

Übung 3

Ersetze das phonetische Symbol [ɑ:] durch das entsprechende orthographische Zeichen.

1 His f[ɑ:]ther was a teacher.
2 Her [ɑ:]nt died last month.
3 The st[ɑ:]ff assembled in the hall.
4 He is always good for a l[ɑ:]gh.
5 The cl[ɑ:]k left for his holidays.
6 He suffered a serious h[ɑ:]t attack.
7 Much h[ɑ:]m is being done to our environment.
8 A g[ɑ:]d was standing at the entrance to the palace.
9 He enjoyed the dr[ɑ:]ma he saw last night.
10 'I'd r[ɑ:]ther have a glass of milk,' he said.

Übung 4

Schreibe die angegebenen Vokale/Diphthonge in die entsprechenden Lücken.

e · ea · ee · ai · oo · o · a · u

1 His father's d☐th came as a terrible shock.
2 There were a lot of d☐d soldiers on the battlefield.
3 That was a gr☐t concert. I liked it very much.
4 They gr☐ted him warmly.
5 There are a lot of p☐rs on the trees this year.
6 This is a very comfortable p☐r of shoes.
7 The string was too l☐se.
8 Don't l☐se your money on the way to the b☐nk.
9 They were resting on a b☐nch.
10 He bought her a lovely b☐nch of flowers.

Übung 5

Setze die orthographischen Zeichen **o** oder **oo** in die entsprechenden Wortlücken ein.

1 The d☐g was barking wildly.
2 He was in a bad m☐d.
3 The d☐r was opened at once.
4 She loved playing with her d☐ll.
5 He l☐ks after his old parents.
6 She has just l☐st her job.
7 A hammer is a useful t☐l.
8 The little boy had to have a t☐th pulled out.
9 They left at n☐n.
10 There is no m☐n tonight.

Übung 6

Setze das phonetische Symbol [e] in die entsprechenden orthographischen Zeichen um.

1 fr[e]nd
2 w[e]pon
3 l[e]ther
4 s[e]d
5 br[e]d
6 d[e]d
7 d[e]f
8 l[e]sure
9 r[e]dy
10 b[e]tter

Übung 7

Schreibe die angegebenen Vokale/Diphthonge in die entsprechenden Lücken.

o · ou · oa · i · ao · e · ui · ea · u · oo · au

1 Gordon Banks was a w☐nderful g☐lkeeper.
2 He w☐nd his clock up.
3 He was sent to g☐l for murder.
4 He fell asleep in the m☐ddle of the talk.
5 Don't m☐ddle in my affairs.
6 The fr☐t this year is particularly j☐cy.
7 He h☐rd his son cry.
8 His broken arm h☐rt him very much.
9 The m☐n was shining brightly.
10 The daily r☐tine proved to be extremely boring.
11 The ☐dience appl☐ded the ☐thor for his excellent book.
12 They took him to c☐rt for theft.

Übung 8

Setze das phonetische Symbol [ʊ] in die entsprechenden orthographischen Zeichen um.

1 p[ʊ]t
2 c[ʊ]shion
3 b[ʊ]som
4 c[ʊ]d
5 f[ʊ]t
6 b[ʊ]sh
7 g[ʊ]d
8 f[ʊ]ll
9 w[ʊ]d
10 s[ʊ]gar

Übung 9

Setze die orthographischen Zeichen **ee** oder **ie** in die Wortlücken ein.

1 Do you want me to p☐l your apple?
2 He bel☐ves in God.
3 We met him in the str☐t.
4 The glass broke into a thousand p☐ces.
5 He p☐ped through the keyhole.
6 I am sure he n☐ds help.
7 My brother's daughter is my n☐ce.
8 He will arrive next w☐k.
9 The pr☐st stepped in front of the altar.
10 The th☐f was caught red-handed.

Übung 10

Setze das phonetische Symbol [i:] in die entsprechenden orthographischen Zeichen um.

1 k[i:]
2 f[i:]d
3 t[i:]th
4 p[i:]ple
5 kn[i:]
6 qu[i:]n
7 gr[i:]ve
8 b[i:]st
9 st[i:]p
10 c[i:]ling

ey · ee · eo · ea · ei · ie

Übung 11

Setze die orthographischen Zeichen in die Wortlücken ein.

1 c☐gh
2 cr☐ss
3 cl☐th
4 kn☐ledge
5 y☐cht
6 fr☐nt
7 l☐rel
8 s☐sage
9 ☐rigin
10 c☐liflower

o · ow · au · ou · a

Übung 12

Setze die orthographischen Zeichen **e** oder **ea** in die Wortlücken ein.

1 He l☐d me through the gate.
2 He had a hat on his h☐d.
3 Give me a slice of br☐d, please.
4 She r☐d the book last night.
5 Her finger bl☐d badly.
6 The murderer fl☐d the country.
7 The kittens were born d☐d.
8 The prince became king after his mother's d☐th.
9 In Great Britain people drive on the l☐ft.
10 He swam two l☐ngths of the pool.

Übung 13

Setze das phonetische Symbol [u:] in die entsprechenden orthographischen Zeichen um.

1 r[u:]de
2 bl[u:]m
3 sh[u:]
4 gr[u:]p
5 wh[u:]se
6 y[u:]th
7 fr[u:]t
8 sh[u:]t
9 S[u:]san
10 w[u:]nd

Übung 14

Setze die entsprechenden orthographischen Zeichen ein.

1 gl☐ve
2 w☐rry
3 st☐dy
4 bl☐dy
5 d☐s
6 fl☐d
7 c☐ntry
8 d☐ll
9 c☐me
10 y☐ng

o · oe · ou · u · oo

Übung 15

Entscheide: **-ible** oder **-able**.

Beispiel: defens☐ = defensible
avoid☐ = avoidable

1 convert☐
2 access☐
3 respons☐
4 suit☐
5 respect☐
6 comfort☐
7 permiss☐
8 cred☐
9 change☐
10 advis☐
11 valu☐
12 unbeliev☐

Übung 16

Füge an die folgenden Wörter die Endungen **-ent** oder **-ant**.

Beispiel: stud□ = student
signific□ = significant

1 innoc□
2 repent□
3 urg□
4 pleas□
5 intellig□
6 const□
7 accid□
8 assist□
9 confid□
10 differ□
11 applic□
12 expect□

Übung 17

Füge an die folgenden Wörter die Endungen **-ence** oder **-ance**.

Beispiel: perform□ = performance
confid□ = confidence

1 annoy□
2 assur□
3 differ□
4 appear□
5 entr□
6 dist□
7 intellig□
8 prud□
9 assist□
10 pres□
11 appli□
12 occurr□
13 griev□
14 experi□
15 evid□
16 insur□
17 utter□
18 depend□

B Die Konsonanten

Es ist kaum möglich, Regeln für die richtige Schreibung der Konsonanten aufzustellen. Die Benutzung eines Lexikons wird sich als unerläßlich erweisen.

Übung 1

Vervollständige die angegebenen Wörter und füge ein: **x** oder **xc**.

Beispiel: e☐act = exact
e☐laim = exclaim

1 e☐ist	**6** e☐it
2 e☐essive	**7** e☐ursion
3 e☐amine	**8** e☐otic
4 e☐use	**9** e☐ess
5 e☐el	**10** e☐eption

Übung 2

Bilde die Vergangenheit der folgenden Formen und achte auf die auslautenden Konsonanten.

Beispiel: beg = begged
sail = sailed

1 plan	**7** consider	**13** refer
2 travel	**8** admit	**14** repel
3 offer	**9** repair	**15** deter
4 stop	**10** plant	**16** trust
5 fail	**11** plead	**17** suffer
6 drop	**12** attempt	**18** level

Übung 3

Setze ein: einfaches oder doppeltes **c, t, d, r, l, n, g**.

1 He was quite su☐essful in his efforts.
2 He failed in his a☐empt to save him.
3 He liked to play with his mo☐el railway.
4 A mi☐or is a glass in which we can see ourselves.
5 She ate her meal in a hu☐y.
6 The tree trunk was ho☐ow.
7 We heard a fu☐y noise.
8 He was as fit as a fi☐le.
9 He could not di☐est the heavy meal.
10 She spent a year at the a☐ademy.

Übung 4

Setze die fehlenden Konsonanten ein, wo nötig.

Beispiel: a☐sure = assure
a☐fraid = afraid

1 a☐plaud	**7** a☐nounce	**13** i☐mature
2 di☐solve	**8** a☐dmire	**14** i☐legal
3 i☐nocent	**9** a☐petite	**15** e☐fort
4 i☐magine	**10** e☐sence	**16** e☐ditor
5 i☐responsible	**11** a☐tach	**17** a☐lways
6 e☐ficient	**12** e☐say	**18** a☐dore

Übung 5

Wann muß das **l** verdoppelt werden?

Beispiel: fulfil☐ed = fulfilled
fail☐ure = failure

1 travel☐er	**4** wel☐fare	**7** wel☐come
2 avail☐able	**5** til☐	**8** al☐ready
3 al☐most	**6** feel☐ing	

Übung 6

Füge an die folgenden Wörter die Konsonanten **c**, **ck** oder **k** an.

Beispiel: wee☐ = week
la☐ = lack

1 lu☐
2 too☐
3 publi☐
4 see☐
5 boo☐
6 kno☐
7 musi☐
8 plasti☐

C Der Plural

Der Plural der Substantive wird im Englischen durch Anfügen von **-s** bzw. **-es** (nach einem Zischlaut) gebildet.
Schwierigkeiten ergeben sich bei Substantiven, die auf **-o** enden, weil der Plural entweder mit **-s** oder **-es** gebildet wird.
Substantive, die auf **-f** enden, bilden den Plural meist auf **-ves**, obwohl es auch Substantive gibt, die im Plural **-fs** haben.
Einige Substantive haben unregelmäßige Pluralformen, d.h. sie bilden den Plural durch Umlaut **(foot – feet)** oder Singular und Plural sind identisch **(sheep – sheep)**, und andere werden nur im Singular gebraucht **(advice, information** u.a.).
Bei den letztgenannten Punkten lassen sich kaum Gesetzmäßigkeiten aufstellen, so daß ein Nachschlagen unerläßlich ist.

Übung 1

Bilde den Plural folgender Wörter.

Beispiel: volcano = volcanoes
radio = radios

1 potato
2 tomato
3 negro
4 piano
5 hero
6 solo
7 tornado
8 mosquito
9 veto
10 buffalo
11 studio
12 photo

"I am sweeping the leaves."

Übung 2

Bilde den Plural folgender Wörter.

Beispiel: roof = roofs
life = lives

1 self	**5** leaf	**9** half
2 loaf	**6** knife	**10** thief
3 calf	**7** wolf	**11** handkerchief
4 wife	**8** scarf	**12** shelf

Übung 3

Bilde den Plural folgender Wörter.

Beispiel: advice = some advice
mouse = mice

1 tooth	**5** man	**9** goose	**13** boy
2 lady	**6** furniture	**10** sheep	**14** foot
3 woman	**7** tray	**11** fish	
4 child	**8** louse	**12** information	

D Das Komma

Der Gebrauch des Kommas ist im Englischen etwas anders als im Deutschen und führt daher oft zu Fehlern. Während das Komma im Deutschen ein Zeichen der Trennung von Satzteilen ist, dient es im Englischen zur Kennzeichnung einer Sprechpause und zur Einteilung des Satzes in Sinngruppen.

Das Komma wird gesetzt:

– bei Aufzählungen.

We had a lesson in geography, biology, English and French.

– zwischen längeren Satzteilen, die u.a. durch **but** oder **though** verbunden sind.

He agreed to accept my suggestion, but I didn't really think he liked it.

– bei Adverbien wie **however, too, of course** oder adverbialen Bestimmungen wie **without success.**

He wanted to come, too.
The children, of course, wanted to have ice-cream.
He tried, without success, to pass his exam.

– vor der wörtlichen Rede.

He said, "How nice of you."

– vor der Jahreszahl bei Datumsangaben in der Reihenfolge Monat, Tag, Jahr.

June 6, 1992

– nach der Anrede und am Schluß von informellen Briefen. Im modernen Briefstil fehlt das Komma hier häufig.

Dear John,
With love,

– nach einem Nebensatz, wenn auf ihn der Hauptsatz folgt.

When you are ready, tell me.

– bei Appositionen.

Jack, our office manager, is ill.

Anders als im Deutschen wird das Komma nicht gesetzt:

– bei notwendigen Relativsätzen.

This is the car he likes most.
Aber: Kommas bei nicht-notwendigen Relativsätzen:
The red car, which he likes most, was stolen.

– vor **that.**

He said that he would come soon.

– vor Subjekt- und Objektsätzen.

It's no wonder that he doesn't agree.
He knew very well what to do.

– vor dem (erweiterten) Infinitiv.

He asked me to help him.

Übung 1

Setze Kommas ein, wo erforderlich.

1 She said "I am glad to meet you."
2 The policeman told me which road to take.
3 The hotel serves excellent breakfasts dinners and teas.
4 The United Kingdom consists of England Wales Scotland and Northern Ireland.
5 Where there is muck there is money.
6 I am sure that he is telling the truth.
7 When he comes home don't forget to give him the money that I owe him.
8 This is the present I bought for her last week.
9 Is this all the money that is left?
10 Before he arrived we had to put everything in order.
11 If however you should not agree we have to find a different solution.
12 She introduced me to her friends most of whom were from England.
13 They moved house on March 31 1990.
14 It's funny that you should think that.
15 When he built his garage his neighbour lent him a hammer a saw and a lot of other tools.

16 He inquired what he was to do.
17 Dear John
Thank you very much for the book which I received before my departure.
With best wishes
Charles
18 John my youngest son has returned from the United States.
19 You too can come if you want to.
20 This was all that he could do for me.
21 Is that the joke you were laughing about?
22 That is exactly the book which I meant.
23 He can read speak and write French and English.
24 "I got my degree last year" Peter remarked.
25 I mentioned that I had seen him before.
26 "May I introduce you to Mr Jones whose son you met at the party last night?"
27 Charles said "Thank you Anne" and went away.
28 My brother however did not pass his exam.
29 If you cannot read it tell me.
30 When he comes give him the book please.
31 Although he was tired he did not go to bed.
32 He nevertheless agreed to what she said.
33 My brother who is a student in London is getting married soon.
34 This is the book which I need for my exam.
35 Peter whose wife is ill cannot come to the concert.

E Die Großschreibung

Mit großen Anfangsbuchstaben werden geschrieben:

- der Satzanfang.

He got up and left.

- das Personalpronomen **I**.

She asked me if I could help her.

- alle Eigennamen und die von ihnen abgeleiteten Adjektive (Personen, Länder, Sprachen, Städte, Feste, Monate, Wochentage, Namen von Parteien).

John, England, English, Manchester, Easter, June, Monday, the Liberals

- Titel, Beinamen, Amtsbezeichnungen.

Professor Johnson, Queen Mary, the Government, the Prime Minister

– alle Wörter mit Ausnahme der Artikel, Präpositionen und Konjunktionen in Überschriften sowie Titeln von Büchern, Filmen, Liedern usw.

God's Little Acre, Elementary Dictionary of English

"That's right! Show everyone that this is our first visit to an Italian restaurant!"

Übung 1

Welche Wörter müssen großgeschrieben werden?

THE LEAST SUCCESSFUL SONG WRITER

for twenty years mr geoffrey o'neill has been writing what he calls 'good catchy tunes that people remember and whistle'. in this time he has composed 501 songs and three musicals. not one of them has been recorded, published or performed by professionals.

mr o'neill, who comes from great dunmow in essex, files all his songs away in case there should be a sudden demand for them. he cheerfully reports that song number 102 is called 'try, try again', while number 332 is entitled 'people think i'm stupid'. an oil firm employee, he gives public lectures on how unsuccessful his songs are.

(Stephen Pile, The Book of Heroic Failures. London, 1979, S. 121)

Übung 2

Schreibe ab und achte auf die Großschreibung.

the united kingdom

the united kingdom is very small compared with many other countries in the world. however, there are only nine other countries with more people, and london is the world's seventh biggest city. the main areas of high land are in scotland, wales and cumbria. in the centre of england is a range of hills called the pennines, which are also known as the 'backbone of england'. the highest mountains are in scotland and wales: ben nevis is 4,406 feet (1,343 m) and snowdon is 3,560 feet (1,085 m). of course, these are very small compared with other mountains in the world – everest, the highest mountain in the world, is 29,000 feet (8,839 m). in fact everything in the united kingdom is rather small – the longest rivers are the severn (220 miles, 354 km) and the river thames (215 miles, 346 km). compare these with the river amazon in south america which is 4,195 miles (6,751 km) long! *(Spotlight on Britain, OUP, 1985, S. 1)*

Übung 3

Schreibe alle Wörter ab, die großgeschrieben werden müssen.

the british system of government
the british parliament consists of the sovereign, the house of lords and the house of commons. the crown makes britain a constitutional monarchy. today the sovereign has no real political power. the queen acts on the advice of the prime minister when she gives her royal assent to bills, dissolves parliament or performs the duties of a head of state. she is also the temporal head of the church of england.
the house of lords consists of over 1000 non-elected members. members can be divided into the lords spiritual, i.e. high bishops of the church of england, and the lords temporal. the latter can be divided into lords who have inherited their titles (hereditary peers), lords who have been given their titles for their own lifetime (life peers), and the law lords. only a relatively small number of the members of the house of lords take an active interest in politics and regularly attend meetings of the house, which usually sits about 145 days each year. the sole power of the house of lords is to delay bills becoming law. the speaker of the house of lords, the lord chancellor, is a member of the cabinet. the law lords sit as the highest court of appeal in england.
the house of commons carries out the bulk of parliamentary work. the 650 members of parliament (mps) who sit in the commons are the elected representatives of the people of the united kingdom (523 for england, 38 for wales, 72 for scotland and 17 for northern ireland). each mp represents one of the 650 constituencies into which the uk is divided. commons has a maximum term of 5 years, at the end of which a general election must be held. however, a general election can be called by the government at any time. a by-election occurs when an mp dies or retires. in each constituency the candidate with the most votes wins; all other votes are lost (first-past-the-post system). today the government's power is concentrated in the hands of one person – the prime minister (pm), who at the same time is the leader of his or her party.

(Britain and America, Cornelsen, 1989, S. 94)

11

Wortschatz

A Homophone

Es gibt im Englischen zahlreiche Wörter, die die gleiche Aussprache haben, aber verschieden geschrieben werden. Sie werden **Homophone** genannt.

Beispiel: **no, know** [nəʊ]

Übung 1

Die einzusetzenden Wörter sind Homophone mit dem Laut [eɪ]. Welches ist das richtige Wort?

1	We □ our sandwiches after the trip. There were □ people in the bus.	**ate/eight**
2	Every single □ in the car must work properly. We had a coffee □ .	**break/brake**
3	She always □ the table in time when she expects guests. Don't □ around, you have work to do.	**lays/laze**
4	He looked very □ . '□' is another word for 'bucket'.	**pail/pale**
5	The □ are at the end of July. This ship has three □ .	**sails/sales**
6	He had to □ for a long time. He was a famous □-lifter.	**wait/weight**
7	A small □ led through the countryside. The policeman said the body had □ there for days.	**lane/lain**
8	He was in terrible □ . The window □ was very dirty.	**pain/pane**

Übung 2

Homophone mit den Lauten [ɑː] und [ɪə]. Welches ist das richtige Wort?

1	You are very naughty, □ you? My □ gave me a lovely birthday present.	**aren't/aunt**
2	He arrived at half □ eight. He □ all his examinations.	**passed/past**
3	Be careful of □ when driving through wooded areas. She was such a □ person.	**dear/deer**

4 Their wedding cake had three □ . **tears/tiers**
□ rolled down her cheeks during the ceremony.
5 Foreigners often mix up the English words '□' and 'listen'. **hear/here**
'□' and 'there' are important words in the English language.

Übung 3

Lies laut und setze die entsprechenden orthographischen Zeichen ein.

1 The w□ther was very promising.
He asked him w□ther he could come.
2 She bought a p□r of shoes.
He likes to eat a juicy p□r for breakfast.
3 The couple walked to the alt□r to get married.
He had to alt□r his plans.
4 Another word for 'lodger' is 'b□rder'.
They were crossing the b□rder.
5 And so on and so f□rth.
He arrived on the f□rth day after Christmas.
6 We left early in the m□rning.
His mother had died. So, he was in m□rning.
7 I w□rn you not to do that.
She has w□rn these shoes for months.
8 She gave b□rth to twins.
My b□rth on the ship was very uncomfortable.
9 It is against the law to de□ert from the army.
He always eats a de□ert after the main course.
10 The plural of 'foot' is 'f□t'.
The engine was a marvellous f□t of engineering.

Übung 4

Homophone mit den Lauten [ɜː], [ɒ], [ʌ], [iː]. Finde das richtige Wort und achte auf die Schreibweise.

1 Some women like wearing □ coats. [fɜː]
□ trees grow in sandy soil.
2 I've got a □ in my shoe lace. [nɒt]
It's □ what you think it is.
3 My uncle only thinks of making a □ in his business. ['prɒfɪt]
Nobody believed what the old □ said.
4 □ and □ make two. [wʌn]
He □ a lot of money in the state lottery.
5 Can I have □ more strawberries, please? [sʌm]
He has just inherited a large □ of money.
6 The □ of her shoe broke as she was going downstairs. [hiːl]
The wound did not □ as quickly as expected.
7 He had to climb in through the window because he couldn't find his □ . [kiː]
After the regatta the yachts were moored at the □ .

8 A □ car is quite common nowadays. The English saying 'Last but not □' is used in countries all over the world. [liːst]

9 The □ of the accident was shown on television. Being □ at parties is very important for the jet set. [siːn]

10 He did not □ a lot of money. 'The Grecian □' is a famous poem. [ɜːn]

Übung 5

Die einzusetzenden Wörter sind Homophone mit dem Laut [ɔː]. Welches ist das richtige Wort?

1 Please □ out your things before we move house. In the past he always □ my advice, but nowadays he makes his own decisions. **sort/sought**

2 The Second World □ lasted for six years. She always □ comfortable shoes. **war/wore**

3 A good book is a □ of delight for me. He eats tomato □ with everything. **sauce/source**

4 He was □ stricken when he saw the tiger. Iron □ is needed to make steel. He lost an □ while rowing. **awe/oar/ore**

5 He was taken to □ for stealing. He was □ by the police. **caught/court**

6 I □ you at the theatre last night. He had a □ throat after shouting so much. **saw/sore**

Übung 6

Homophone mit dem Laut [eə]. Welches Wort muß eingesetzt werden?

1 □ on earth have you been? Some people □ clothes for warmth, others for fun. **wear/where**

2 A □ is like a rabbit, but it is larger and has long ears. Her mother didn't want her to have her □ cut. **hair/hare**

3 The pain was almost more than he could □ . The teacher only wanted to have the □ facts. **bare/bear**

4 People think of Germans as being tall and □ . The □ from London to Los Angeles is very expensive. **fair/fare**

5 A □ is a fruit which grows on trees. This □ of shoes is too expensive. **pair/pear**

6 There's dust here, □ and everywhere. The children always got □ pocket money on Mondays. □ never in, but always out. **their/there/they're**

Übung 7

Homophone mit dem Laut [aɪ]. Finde das richtige Wort und achte auf die Schreibweise.

1 A building □ in the neighbourhood is unpleasant for the residents. [saɪt]
The □ of his newborn baby was overwhelming for him.

2 Which answer is □ and which is wrong? [raɪt]
Don't forget to □ down your name and address.

3 In Great Britain one drives on the left-hand □. [saɪd]
The passengers □ with relief when the plane landed safely.

4 The bride's parents wanted to □ a Rolls Royce for the wedding. ['haɪə]
Mt. Everest is □ than Mt. Blanc.

5 □ be with you in a while. [aɪl]
The □ of Skye is off the Scottish coast.

6 My brother is going to □ a new house. [baɪ]
I never like saying good □.

Übung 8

Lies laut und setze die entsprechenden orthographischen Zeichen ein.

1 Instead of 'to escape' you can also say 'to fl□'.
He was bitten by a fl□.

2 The h□ls came off her shoes.
This is a wound which h□ls quickly.

3 We had some tasty m□t for dinner.
Let's m□t at seven o'clock.

4 All nations long for p□ce.
This was a wonderful p□ce of music.

5 You must not st□l.
Machinery is usually made of st□l.

6 His illness made him very w□k.
He will be here in a w□k.

"Oh, no! – not another! And they aren't even a pair!"

Übung 9

Homophone mit dem Laut [uː]. Welches Wort muß eingesetzt werden?

1 ☐ and ☐ make four. **too/two**
This piece of furniture is ☐ heavy for me to lift.

2 ☐ car are you going in? **who's/whose**
☐ the boss here, you or me?

3 We have a ☐ boy in our class. **knew/new**
I ☐ he was the thief.

4 I like walking in the morning ☐. **dew/due**
He lost his job ☐ to his unpunctuality.

5 The referee ☐ his whistle. **blew/blue**
My husband has ☐ eyes.

6 The landlord ☐ the student out because he hadn't paid the rent. **threw/through**
We passed ☐ Holland on our way to Germany.

Übung 10

Homophone mit dem Laut [əʊ]. Finde das richtige Wort und achte auf seine Schreibweise.

1 The king's son is heir to the ☐. [θrəʊn]
So much food is ☐ away nowadays.

2 I didn't ☐ you knew each other. [nəʊ]
My little boy says '☐' to everything.

3 My son was so hungry that he ate a ☐ loaf of bread. [həʊl]
There's a ☐ in the sleeve of my pullover.

4 I enjoy eating a crispy ☐ for breakfast. [rəʊl]
He had played an active ☐ in community life.

5 I am conscious of my big ☐. [nəʊz]
He thinks he ☐ everything.

6 He is always the heart and ☐ of parties. [səʊl]
My ☐ reason for going to France is to learn French.

Übung 11

Homophone mit dem Laut [eɪ]. Setze das richtige Wort ein.

1 She had to ask the ☐ to the station. **weigh/way**
Some people ☐ themselves every day.

2 We had a lot of ☐ last month. **rain/reign**
During the ☐ of Elizabeth II Great Britain became a member of the Common Market.

3 The beauty queen had a very slim ☐. **waste/waist**
Ships throw their ☐ into the sea.

4 The dog wagged its ☐. **tail/tale**
He told me a funny ☐.

5 The ☐ was delayed by fog. **plain/plane**
He preferred ☐ bread and butter for breakfast.

Übung 12

Homophone mit dem Laut [e]. Finde das richtige Wort. Beachte seine Schreibweise.

1 Most German houses have a □ . ['selə]
'□' is the opposite of buyer.
2 I enjoy getting □ in the rain. [wet]
A glass of sherry is supposed to □ your appetite.
3 □ is a very dangerous drug. ['herəʊm]
There's always a hero or a □ in adventure books.
4 They went up the mountain by cable car and made the □ on foot. [dɪ'sent]
There was always a lot of □ in the office.
5 Children must not play with toys containing □ . [led]
He □ the little boy by the hand.

B Homonyme

Wörter, die gleich lauten und auch gleich geschrieben werden, aber eine andere Bedeutung haben, nennt man **Homonyme.**

Beispiel: **bark** = „bellen" und „Baumrinde"

Übung 1

Setze die angegebenen Wörter in die entsprechenden Lücken ein.

alight · ball · box · blow · spell · issue · bank · called

1 People should not □ from a bus until it has stopped.
2 She had to □ on her tea to cool it down.
3 He took his money to the □ .
4 He put his books in a large □ .
5 He □ the players' names.
6 The player kicked the □ into the goal.
7 This □ will be discussed next week.
8 How do you □ your name?
9 We always do something special at New Year. This year we are going to a □ .
10 Their faces were □ with joy.
11 The Dogger □ in the North Sea is good for fishing.
12 Yesterday's □ of our daily newspaper was boring.
13 Did you □ at school? – No, I hated fighting.
14 I □ the doctor because my son wasn't very well in the night.
15 His father's death was a terrible □ for him.
16 Last summer we had a □ of bad weather.

Übung 2

Setze folgende Wörter ein.

fine · draw · fast · kind · clear · match

1 She was ☐ asleep.
2 He discovered a new ☐ of insect.
3 Please, ☐ the curtains properly.
4 Did you enjoy the football ☐ this afternoon?
5 We found him very friendly and ☐ .
6 He is a ☐ musician, indeed.
7 The game ended in a ☐ .
8 He took a ☐ out of his matchbox and lit his cigar.
9 He had to pay a high ☐ for breaking the law.
10 He ran as ☐ as he could.
11 His instructions were very ☐ .
12 Your room looks very untidy. Don't expect me to ☐ it up.

Übung 3

Welche Wörter gehören in die Lücken?

case · fell · light · tell · like · long · present · race

1 He could not see properly due to the bad ☐ .
2 Can you ☐ me the way to the station, please?
3 There was a ☐ break after the first act of the drama.
4 She came third in the horse ☐ .
5 The ☐ headmaster is a very nice gentleman.
6 They looked ☐ brother and sister.
7 They both look alike. I can never ☐ one from the other.
8 His ☐ will come up at court soon.
9 I ☐ down and broke my arm.
10 I only want one ☐ for my birthday.
11 He belongs to a different ☐ .
12 After a cold winter people ☐ for the warmth of spring.
13 We ☐ classical music.
14 Last night's thunderstorm was only a ☐ one.
15 The patient was an urgent ☐ and was operated on immediately.
16 It is dangerous for the environment to ☐ too many trees.

C Homographe

Wörter, die gleich geschrieben werden, deren Lautung aber verschieden ist, werden als **Homographe** bezeichnet.

Beispiel: **tear** = [tɪə] und [teə]

Übung 1

Setze die entsprechenden Wörter in die Lücken ein. Achte auf die Wörter in den Kästchen.

1 He ☐ his genius to his grandparents. The headmaster thought the teacher had a lot of ☐ .	**a**ttributes attr**i**butes
2 One must ☐ intelligence with wit. The farmer was proud of his ☐ harvester.	c**o**mbine comb**i**ne
3 His ☐ was excellent. He was asked to ☐ the school orchestra.	cond**u**ct c**o**nduct
4 The children were not ☐ with his will. He was not satisfied with the ☐ of the essay.	c**o**ntent cont**e**nt
5 They signed the ☐ at the lawyer's office. I hope I won't ☐ malaria in Africa.	c**o**ntract contr**a**ct

Übung 2

Lies laut und achte auf die hervorgehobenen Wörter.

1 The Sahara is the biggest DESERT in the world.
The officer hoped the soldiers would not DESERT.

2 Some food is difficult to DIGEST.
He compiled a DIGEST of stories.

3 I hope they will not EXPLOIT him at the office.
He climbed Mount Everest. What an EXPLOIT.

4 The novelist read an EXTRACT from his book.
The dentist had to EXTRACT two teeth.

5 His FREQUENT visits are a nuisance.
They FREQUENT bars when they are on holiday.

6 The professor was a LEARNED scholar.
I LEARNED Italian in Italy.

7 He LIVES in Africa.
A cat is said to have nine LIVES.

8 He has a little boy AGED five.
He is an AGED, old man.

Übung 3

Lies und entscheide dich für eine der angebotenen Möglichkeiten.

1	Silicon chips for a computer are ☐ .	**minute** [maɪ'nju:t, 'mɪnɪt]
2	They had a ☐ about pocket money.	**row** [raʊ, rəʊ]
3	Female pigs are ☐ .	**sows** [saʊz, səʊz]
4	He did not shed a ☐ at the funeral.	**tear** [tɪə, teə]
5	I am ☐ to the hot climate.	**used** [ju:st, ju:zd]
6	The ☐ blew strongly yesterday.	**wind** [wɪnd, waɪnd]
7	His ☐ was very serious.	**wound** [wu:nd, waʊnd]
8	I have never ☐ a computer before.	**used** [ju:st, ju:zd]
9	There was a small ☐ in my new dress.	**tear** [tɪə, teə]
10	I like sitting in the last ☐ at the theatre.	**row** [raʊ, rəʊ]
11	The farmer ☐ his seeds at the same time every year.	**sows** [saʊz, səʊz]
12	Just a ☐ . I'm almost ready.	**minute** [maɪ'nju:t, 'mɪnɪt]
13	It's very ☐ and thundery today.	**close** [kləʊs, kləʊz]
14	He always ☐ to the audience at the end of a performance.	**bows** [baʊz, bəʊz]
15	He ☐ the clock every evening.	**wound** [wu:nd, waʊnd]
16	Please ☐ the door.	**close** [kləʊs, kləʊz]
17	In the Middle Ages ☐ and arrows were used.	**bows** [baʊz, bəʊz]
18	You must ☐ your watch regularly.	**wind** [wɪnd, waɪnd]

"You know that 24-piece tea-set we had as a wedding present, dear? . . . Well, I'm afraid I've increased it to about two hundred."

Übung 4

Setze die entsprechenden Wörter in die Lücken ein. Achte auf die unterschiedliche Betonung.

1 I ☐ to you smoking. — **o**bject/obj**e**ct
She was the ☐ of his interest.

2 What ☐ can I give you for your birthday? — pr**e**sent/pres**e**nt
May I ☐ Mr Johnson?

3 They always sell their ☐ at the market. — prod**u**ce/pr**o**duce
Shall we ☐ the play together?

4 His ☐ was a hit. — r**e**cord/rec**o**rd
Let's ☐ the concert.

5 The amount of ☐ increases from year to year. — r**e**fuse/ref**u**se
I ☐ to lend you any more money.

6 Are you ☐ to colds? — s**u**bject/subj**e**ct
They did not want to ☐ him to torture.

D Synonyme

Ein deutsches Wort – mehrere Begriffe im Englischen.
Für den gleichen deutschen Oberbegriff steht im Englischen oft ein Wort germanischen bzw. romanischen Ursprungs. Diese Wörter sind allerdings nie völlig synonym, sondern haben feine Bedeutungsunterschiede.
Das deutsche Wort „Fleisch" wird beispielsweise wiedergegeben mit dem Wort **meat**, wenn es sich um tierisches, aber mit **flesh**, wenn es sich um menschliches Fleisch handelt. Ebenso wird ein **sheep** (Schaf) zum **mutton**, wenn es gegessen wird. Ein anderes Beispiel ist das deutsche Wort „bringen", das im Englischen je nach Situation mit **bring** oder **take** übersetzt werden muß.

Die folgenden Übungen greifen diese Problematik auf, wobei jedoch auf solche Synonyme verzichtet wird, deren Bedeutungsunterschiede durch häufigen Gebrauch so verwischt sind, daß kaum noch Unterschiede bestehen.

Für alle Übungen gilt: Setze das richtige Wort ein und beachte dabei die notwendigen Änderungen.

all – quite – whole

1 Tell me the ☐ truth.
2 He knew ☐ the time that something was wrong.
3 The ☐ team was exhausted after the match.
4 This book is ☐ good.
5 ☐ the glasses were broken.

alter – change

1 When he lost weight he had to have his suits ☐ .
2 Why have you ☐ your opinion?
3 He left the seaside resort when the weather began to ☐ .
4 You have to ☐ these trousers. They are too tight.
5 It is always difficult to ☐ old people's habits.

ancient – elderly – old

1 She is highly interested in ☐ history.
2 He is twelve years ☐ .
3 ☐ English is completely different from Modern English.
4 The library was run by an ☐ lady.
5 There is a new home for the ☐ near us.

attend – visit

1 Have you ever ☐ New York?
2 He ☐ a very expensive boarding school when he was a child.
3 When he is in London, he always ☐ concerts at the Royal Albert Hall.
4 You must ☐ the Louvre when you are in Paris.
5 My brother has to ☐ lectures every day.

bear – carry – wear

1 I can never find a porter to ☐ my luggage.
2 What on earth shall I ☐ to my sister's wedding?
3 He has to ☐ glasses when he is driving.
4 Is the ice thick enough to ☐ your weight?
5 I have to ☐ the responsibility for the new project.
6 The little girl always wanted her mother to ☐ her.

boil – cook

1 Water ☐ at 100 °C.
2 She always has a soft-☐ egg for breakfast.
3 She hates being in the kitchen and does not like ☐ at all.
4 The man could ☐, but his wife could not.
5 To make a good cup of tea, you must ☐ the water.

borrow – lend

1 I ☐ this book from the library last week.
2 Please ☐ me your pen. I have lost mine.
3 May I ☐ your lawn mower? Mine is broken.
4 Jane promised to ☐ me her bike at the weekend.
5 I really do not want to ☐ him any more money.

bottom – floor – ground

1 They could not finish the game because the ☐ was so muddy.
2 He slipped on the bathroom ☐ .
3 You are on dangerous ☐ when you criticize his work.
4 There was a hole in the ☐ of the box.
5 The wreck was lying at the ☐ of the sea.

"Did we bring the baby to the shops?"

bring – take

1 "☐ the boxes to the attic," she shouted from the kitchen.
2 The minister asked who could ☐ the old lady home.
3 Would you ☐ us another bottle of wine, please?
4 When you come at the weekend, don't forget to ☐ your holiday photos.
5 My husband will ☐ you to the airport.

bring up – educate

1 When her parents died, she was ☐ by her aunt and uncle.
2 It is not easy to ☐ children to be polite.
3 He was ☐ at private schools.
4 Schools need qualified teachers to ☐ children.
5 Her husband died very young, so she had to ☐ the children alone.

canal – channel

1 The ☐ Islands are famous holiday resorts.
2 The Suez ☐ is one of the most important waterways in the world.
3 Irrigation ☐ help to water desert areas.
4 The news is transmitted hourly on ☐ six.
5 A ☐ is always man-made.
6 There will soon be a tunnel under the English ☐ .

cause – reason

1 The ☐ of the fire was a cigarette.
2 The ☐ why he could not come was obvious.
3 She could not explain to the police what the ☐ of the accident was.
4 My mother's health is giving me ☐ for concern.
5 You have no ☐ for being late.

colour – paint

1 The sign read 'Wet ☐' .
2 The building is so old that the ☐ is coming off.
3 He could still remember the evening he saw the first ☐ film.
4 The doctor diagnosed that he was ☐-blind.
5 He had to buy a new tin of ☐ .
6 What ☐ are your eyes?

company – society

1 He works for a large insurance ☐ .
2 I enjoy my mother-in-law's ☐ .
3 Careless drivers are a constant danger to ☐ .
4 We live in a multi-racial ☐ .
5 You are often judged by the ☐ you keep.

country – land

1 He was very proud of his ☐ .
2 He planned to build a big house on his own ☐ .
3 Spain is a ☐ in Western Europe.
4 When he won a lot of money he bought a ☐ house.
5 In some places ☐ is more expensive than in other places.
6 Life in the ☐ is healthier than in the town.

deserve – earn

1 How do you ☐ your living?
2 Did he really ☐ the treatment he got?
3 She had a salary rise and now ☐ more than her father.
4 They ☐ recognition for all the work they have done.
5 She doesn't ☐ to be punished.

detect – discover

1 Columbus ☐ America in 1492.
2 Last night the police ☐ the theft too late to catch the burglar.
3 Little children ☐ new things every day.
4 Modern submarines can hardly be ☐ by the enemy's technology.
5 The device ☐ any kind of metal.

difficult – heavy

1 The question was ☐ to answer.
2 My mother is not allowed to carry ☐ things.
3 Physics has always been a ☐ subject for him.
4 He has a ☐ cold.
5 It is ☐ to know what we should do.

do – make

1 I cannot come to the cinema this evening because I have got too much homework to ☐ .
2 I am very sorry, but I really cannot ☐ an exception to the rule.
3 What does he ☐ for a living?
4 What do you normally ☐ at weekends?
5 If you are not careful, you will ☐ a mistake.

drive – go – ride

1 I normally ☐ my bike to work.
2 Please be careful when you ☐ our new car.
3 He has never ☐ to work by taxi.
4 As the traffic is so heavy, I think it would be better to ☐ by bus.
5 Can I ☐ you to the station?

end – stop

1 World War I ☐ in November 1918.
2 They ☐ playing cards when the telephone rang.
3 The last match ☐ in a draw.
4 The meeting ☐ in confusion half an hour ago.
5 The teacher told the pupils to ☐ talking.

false – wrong

1 You have taken the ☐ key.
2 Whatever you do, it is bound to be ☐ .
3 You must never give ☐ evidence.
4 Is the answer true or ☐ ?
5 Please don't get me ☐ . I am not criticizing you.
6 The dentist told him he would have to have ☐ teeth.

fault – mistake

1 He speaks English quite fluently, but still makes a lot of grammar ☐ .
2 He made a big ☐ when he thought he could trust her.
3 You can learn from your ☐ .
4 She liked him very much in spite of his ☐ .
5 If she hadn't made so many spelling ☐ she would have passed the exam.
6 The policeman told him that the accident was his ☐ .

finished – ready

1 The ☐ product was expensive.
2 Wash your hands, please. Dinner is almost ☐ .
3 He smiled when he looked at the ☐ painting.
4 We are almost ☐ to leave.
5 Everything is ☐ for the journey.

flesh – meat

1 The ☐ was nice and tender and the guests enjoyed the meal immensely.
2 He was my own ☐ and blood.
3 The tool slipped and went deep into his ☐ .
4 He likes his ☐ well-done.
5 The price for ☐ is constantly going up.

float – swim

1 Does a cork ☐ or sink?
2 The boat was damaged and did not ☐ .
3 She ☐ like a fish.
4 Let's go for a ☐ .
5 He ☐ a new world record yesterday.

force – power – strength

1 France has more nuclear ☐ stations than any other European country.
2 These rules are in ☐ for the next few months.
3 He tried to open the door by ☐ .
4 The hungry man didn't have the ☐ to lift anything.
5 He was the driving ☐ behind the project.

foreign – strange

1 I like travelling to ☐ countries.
2 He had ☐ ideas about religion.
3 Mr James is the new minister for ☐ affairs.
4 I had a ☐ feeling that you would say that.
5 It is ☐ that you should mention this.

gain – win

1 They are an excellent team. So, they were bound to ☐ .
2 This will give you the chance to ☐ relevant experience.
3 He always ☐ at cards.
4 John ☐ the first prize for biology last year.
5 After a nervous start, the speaker began to ☐ confidence.
6 After a strenuous ninety minutes the team ☐ 3:0.

game – match – play

1 Hockey is a popular ☐ in Great Britain.
2 I enjoy watching a tennis ☐ on TV.
3 Bridge is a difficult card ☐ .
4 Steve Smith was sent off during the football final for unfair ☐ .
5 Anybody can do it. It is child's ☐ .

get up – stand up

1 I always ☐ at 6 o'clock.
2 The old lady fell down and could not ☐ without help.
3 The audience ☐ when the national anthem was played.
4 He ☐ so that he could see better.
5 Hurry up! It is time to ☐, otherwise you will be late for school.

go – walk

1 It is very late. I'm afraid I must ☐ now.
2 It is healthy to ☐ a few miles every day.
3 The weather is beautiful. Let's ☐ to the shops rather than take the bus.
4 Time seems to ☐ so quickly.
5 How do you ☐ to work – by bus or by car?

happy – lucky

1 They always seemed so ☐ together. Everyone was surprised when they said they were getting divorced.
2 He had an accident, but was very ☐ and got away with minor injuries.
3 Money does not always make people ☐ .
4 He was ☐ and won in the lottery.
5 He seems to be such a ☐ person; he always gets away with everything.

"Look. He is happy, because you have come home."

hear – listen to

1 We ☐ the brakes screeching, but we could not prevent the crash.
2 Have you ☐ the latest score?
3 I usually ☐ the radio when I am having my breakfast.
4 I have never ☐ of that restaurant. Where is it?
5 She often ☐ music in the evenings.

husband – man

1 They wanted a ☐, not a woman for this job.
2 He is a model ☐ to his wife.
3 The diplomat was a ☐ of the world.
4 She has just got divorced from her second ☐ .
5 I have never met my friend's ☐ even though they have been married for over two years.

job – labour – work

1 This wardrobe is really a ☐ of art.
2 When his work became boring he decided to change his ☐ .
3 The ☐ Party has lost a lot of its former power.
4 ☐ Day is a public holiday.
5 His firm went bankrupt, so he lost his ☐ .

journey – travel

1 Package holidays can be booked at a ☐ agency.
2 Have a good ☐!
3 Do you suffer from ☐ sickness?
4 The ☐ to Australia took over 24 hours.
5 We did half the ☐ by ship and half by plane.

little – small

1 He only had a ☐ income to support his large family.
2 We had ☐ chance of success.
3 In comparison to her old garden, her new one is rather ☐ .
4 I want to make a phone call. Have you got any ☐ change, please?
5 This is of ☐ importance.

need - use

1 May I ☐ your pen? I've lost mine.
2 Don't you see that he ☐ help?
3 She could not ☐ it because it was completely broken.
4 There is no ☐ to be afraid.
5 They desperately ☐ money to pay the rent.

occupation – profession – trade

1 He is a carpenter by ☐ .
2 The legal ☐ has a great responsibility.
3 He is a highly skilled craftsman and knows all about his ☐ .
4 After studying at university he wanted to go into the medical ☐ .
5 Please state your name, age and ☐ .

policy – politics

1 Anybody can go into ☐ . The main thing is that you are able to talk.
2 Do you know much about German ☐ ?
3 His present ☐ will get us nowhere.
4 He is very active in local ☐ .
5 Gandhi's ☐ of non-violence led to success.

price – prize

1 The ☐ he had to pay was very high.
2 He received the first ☐ for his efforts.
3 I refuse to pay such an exorbitant ☐ .
4 The book is not worth the ☐ I had to pay for it.
5 This year's Nobel ☐ winner was from Norway.

remember - remind

1 I cannot ☐ what you said.
2 He ☐ me of his brother.
3 Please try to ☐ what you saw at the scene of the accident.
4 I cannot ☐ the name of the place.
5 Please ☐ me to go to the bank.

rob – steal

1 The bank robbers got away in a car they had ☐ .
2 The thieves ☐ the jeweller of his most precious jewels last night.
3 When they travelled through the city, they were ☐ in broad daylight.
4 In a bank raid more than £2 million were ☐ .
5 The bank has been ☐ several times over the last few months.
6 During the night his car was broken into and the radio ☐ .

say – tell

1 Don't ☐ me what I should do all the time.
2 What did your brother ☐ when he phoned?
3 ☐ him to stop singing so loudly.
4 He did not ☐ where he was going to spend his holidays.
5 ☐ what you think and you will not be sorry.
6 ☐ me what happened at the pub last night.

shade – shadow

1 We rested in the ☐ of a tree.
2 The sun shone on them and they couldn't find any ☐ .
3 The detective followed him like a ☐ .
4 It was over 30 degrees in the ☐ yesterday.
5 He is a ☐ of his former self.

wife – woman

1 She was a ☐ of the world and admired by everybody.
2 A ☐ cannot become a priest in the Catholic church.
3 She is his second ☐ . He got divorced from his first in 1985.
4 She was a good ☐ and mother.
5 One ☐ did all the work.

Liste der unregelmäßigen Verben

arise [ə'raɪz]	arose [ə'rəʊz]	arisen [ə'rɪzn]	*sich erheben*
awake [ə'weɪk]	awoke [ə'wəʊk]	awoken [ə'wəʊkən]	*erwachen*
be [bi:]	was [wɒz]	been [bi:n]	*sein*
bear [beə(r)]	bore [bɔ:(r)]	borne [bɔ:n]	*ertragen*
bear [beə(r)]	bore [bɔ:(r)]	born [bɔ:n]	*gebären*
beat [bi:t]	beat [bi:t]	beaten ['bi:tn]	*schlagen*
become [bɪ'kʌm]	became [bɪ'keɪm]	become [bɪ'kʌm]	*werden*
begin [bɪ'gɪn]	began [bɪ'gæn]	begun [bɪ'gʌn]	*beginnen, anfangen*
bend [bend]	bent [bent]	bent [bent]	*beugen, biegen*
bet [bet]	bet [bet]	bet [bet]	*wetten*
bid [bɪd]	bade [beɪd]	bidden ['bɪdn]	*heißen, gebieten*
bid [bɪd]	bid [bɪd]	bid [bɪd]	*bieten (Preis)*
bind [baɪnd]	bound [baʊnd]	bound [baʊnd]	*binden*
bite [baɪt]	bit [bɪt]	bit(ten) ['bɪtn]	*beißen*
bleed [bli:d]	bled [bled]	bled [bled]	*bluten*
blow [bləʊ]	blew [blu:]	blown [bləʊn]	*blasen*
break [breɪk]	broke [brəʊk]	broken ['brəʊkən]	*zerbrechen*
breed [bri:d]	bred [bred]	bred [bred]	*brüten; züchten*
bring [brɪŋ]	brought [brɔ:t]	brought [brɔ:t]	*bringen*
broadcast ['brɔ:dkɑ:st]	broadcast ['brɔ:dkɑ:st]	broadcast ['brɔ:dkɑ:st]	*(im Rundfunk) senden*
build [bɪld]	built [bɪlt]	built [bɪlt]	*bauen*
burn [bɜ:n]	burnt [bɜ:nt]	burnt [bɜ:nt]	*(ver)brennen*
burst [bɜ:st]	burst [bɜ:st]	burst [bɜ:st]	*bersten; platzen*
buy [baɪ]	bought [bɔ:t]	bought [bɔ:t]	*kaufen*
cast [kɑ:st]	cast [kɑ:st]	cast [kɑ:st]	*werfen; gießen (Metall)*
catch [kætʃ]	caught [kɔ:t]	caught [kɔ:t]	*fangen*
choose [tʃu:z]	chose [tʃəʊz]	chosen ['tʃəʊzn]	*wählen; (sich) aussuchen*
cling [klɪŋ]	clang [klæŋ]	clung [klʌŋ]	*sich (an)klammern*
come [kʌm]	came [keɪm]	come [kʌm]	*kommen*
cost [kɒst]	cost [kɒst]	cost [kɒst]	*kosten*
creep [kri:p]	crept [krept]	crept [krept]	*kriechen*
cut [kʌt]	cut [kʌt]	cut [kʌt]	*schneiden*
deal [di:l]	dealt [delt]	dealt [delt]	*handeln, sich befassen mit*
dig [dɪg]	dug [dʌg]	dug [dʌg]	*graben*
do [du:]	did [dɪd]	done [dʌn]	*tun*
draw [drɔ:]	drew [dru:]	drawn [drɔ:n]	*ziehen, zeichnen*
dream [dri:m]	dreamt [dremt] dreamed [dri:md]	dreamt [dremt] dreamed [dri:md]	*träumen*
drink [drɪŋk]	drank [dræŋk]	drunk [drʌŋk]	*trinken*
drive [draɪv]	drove [drəʊv]	driven ['drɪvn]	*treiben, fahren*
dwell [dwel]	dwelt [dwelt]	dwelt [dwelt]	*(ver)weilen; wohnen*
eat [i:t]	ate [et/eɪt]	eaten ['i:tn]	*essen*
fall [fɔ:l]	fell [fel]	fallen ['fɔ:lən]	*fallen*
feed [fi:d]	fed [fed]	fed [fed]	*füttern*
feel [fi:l]	felt [felt]	felt [felt]	*(sich) fühlen*

fight [faɪt]	fought [fɔːt]	fought [fɔːt]	*kämpfen*
find [faɪnd]	found [faʊnd]	found [faʊnd]	*finden*
flee [fliː]	fled [fled]	fled [fled]	*fliehen*
fling [flɪŋ]	flung [flʌŋ]	flung [flʌŋ]	*schleudern, werfen*
fly [flaɪ]	flew [fluː]	flown [fləʊn]	*fliegen*
forbid [fə'bɪd]	forbad(e) [fə'bæd, -eɪ-]	forbidden [fə'bɪdn]	*verbieten*
forecast ['fɔːkɑːst]	forecast ['fɔːkɑːst]	forecast ['fɔːkɑːst]	*vorhersagen (Wetter)*
	forecasted ['fɔːkɑːstɪd]	forecasted ['fɔːkɑːstɪd]	
forget [fə'get]	forgot [fə'gɒt]	forgotten [fə'gɒtn]	*vergessen*
forgive [fə'gɪv]	forgave [fə'geɪv]	forgiven [fə'gɪvn]	*vergeben, verzeihen*
freeze [friːz]	froze [frəʊz]	frozen ['frəʊzn]	*(ge)frieren, erfrieren*
get [get]	got [gɒt]	got [gɒt]	*bekommen, werden*
give [gɪv]	gave [geɪv]	given ['gɪvn]	*geben*
go [gəʊ]	went [went]	gone [gɒn]	*gehen*
grind [graɪnd]	ground [graʊnd]	ground [graʊnd]	*mahlen*
grow [grəʊ]	grew [gruː]	grown [grəʊn]	*wachsen; anbauen*
have [hæv]	had [hæd]	had [hæd]	*haben*
hear [hɪə]	heard [hɜːd]	heard [hɜːd]	*hören*
hide [haɪd]	hid [hɪd]	hidden ['hɪdn]	*verbergen, (sich) verstecken*
hit [hɪt]	hit [hɪt]	hit [hɪt]	*schlagen; hauen; treffen*
hold [həʊld]	held [held]	held [held]	*halten*
hurt [hɜːt]	hurt [hɜːt]	hurt [hɜːt]	*verletzen; weh tun*
keep [kiːp]	kept [kept]	kept [kept]	*(be)halten, verweilen bei*
kneel [niːl]	knelt [nelt]	knelt [nelt]	*knien*
knit [nɪt]	knit [nɪt]	knit [nɪt]	*stricken*
	knitted ['nɪtɪd]	knitted ['nɪtɪd]	
know [nəʊ]	knew [njuː]	known [nəʊn]	*kennen, wissen*
lay [leɪ]	laid [leɪd]	laid [leɪd]	*legen; (Tisch) decken*
lead [liːd]	led [led]	led [led]	*leiten, führen*
lean [liːn]	leant [lent]	leant [lent]	*lehnen*
	leaned [liːnd]	leaned [liːnd]	
leap [liːp]	leapt [lept]	leapt [lept]	*hüpfen; springen*
	leaped [liːpt]	leaped [liːpt]	
learn [lɜːn]	learnt [lɜːnt]	learnt [lɜːnt]	*lernen; erfahren*
	learned [lɜːnd]	learned [lɜːnd]	
leave [liːv]	left [left]	left [left]	*(ver)lassen; zurücklassen, weggehen*
lend [lend]	lent [lent]	lent [lent]	*leihen*
let [let]	let [let]	let [let]	*lassen; vermieten*
lie [laɪ]	lay [leɪ]	lain [leɪn]	*liegen*
light [laɪt]	lit [lɪt]	lit [lɪt]	*anzünden, erleuchten*
	lighted ['laɪtɪd]	lighted ['laɪtɪd]	
lose [luːz]	lost [lɒst]	lost [lɒst]	*verlieren*
make [meɪk]	made [meɪd]	made [meɪd]	*machen*
mean [miːn]	meant [ment]	meant [ment]	*meinen, bedeuten*
meet [miːt]	met [met]	met [met]	*begegnen, (sich) treffen*
mistake [mɪ'steɪk]	mistook [mɪ'stʊk]	mistaken [mɪ'steɪkən]	*verwechseln*
mow [məʊ]	mowed [məʊd]	mown [məʊn]	*mähen*
pay [peɪ]	paid [peɪd]	paid [peɪd]	*(be)zahlen*
put [pʊt]	put [pʊt]	put [pʊt]	*setzen; legen; stellen*

quit [kwɪt]	quit [kwɪt]	quit [kwɪt]	*aufgeben; aufhören,*
	quitted ['kwɪtɪd]	quitted ['kwɪtɪd]	*verlassen*
read [riːd]	read [red]	read [red]	*lesen*
ride [raɪd]	rode [rəʊd]	ridden ['rɪdn]	*reiten, fahren*
ring [rɪŋ]	rang [ræŋ]	rung [rʌŋ]	*läuten; anrufen (Telefon)*
rise [raɪz]	rose [rəʊz]	risen ['rɪzn]	*aufstehen*
run [rʌn]	ran [ræn]	run [rʌn]	*rennen; laufen*
saw [sɔː]	sawed [sɔːd]	sawn [sɔːn]	*sägen*
		sawed [sɔːd]	
say [seɪ]	said [sed]	said [sed]	*sagen*
see [siː]	saw [sɔː]	seen [siːn]	*sehen*
seek [siːk]	sought [sɔːt]	sought [sɔːt]	*suchen*
sell [sel]	sold [səʊld]	sold [səʊld]	*verkaufen*
send [send]	sent [sent]	sent [sent]	*senden; verschicken*
set [set]	set [set]	set [set]	*setzen; stellen; untergehen*
			(Sonne)
sew [səʊ]	sewed [səʊd]	sewn [səʊn]	*nähen*
shake [ʃeɪk]	shook [ʃʊk]	shaken ['ʃeɪkən]	*schütteln*
shine [ʃaɪn]	shone [ʃɒn]	shone [ʃɒn]	*scheinen, glänzen*
shoot [ʃuːt]	shot [ʃɒt]	shot [ʃɒt]	*(er)schießen*
show [ʃəʊ]	showed [ʃəʊd]	shown [ʃəʊn]	*zeigen*
	showed [ʃəʊd]	showed [ʃəʊd]	
shrink [ʃrɪŋk]	shrank [ʃræŋk]	shrunk [ʃrʌŋk]	*schrumpfen,*
			zurückschrecken
shut [ʃʌt]	shut [ʃʌt]	shut [ʃʌt]	*schließen, zumachen*
sing [sɪŋ]	sang [sæŋ]	sung [sʌŋ]	*singen*
sink [sɪŋk]	sank [sæŋk]	sunk [sʌŋk]	*sinken*
sit [sɪt]	sat [sæt]	sat [sæt]	*sitzen*
sleep [sliːp]	slept [slept]	slept [slept]	*schlafen*
speak [spiːk]	spoke [spəʊk]	spoken ['spəʊkən]	*sprechen*
speed [spiːd]	sped [sped]	sped [sped]	*sich beeilen, schnell fahren*
	speeded ['spiːdɪd]	speeded ['spiːdɪd]	
spell [spel]	spelt [spelt]	spelt [spelt]	*buchstabieren*
	spelled [speld]	spelled [speld]	
spend [spend]	spent [spent]	spent [spent]	*verbringen (Zeit);*
			ausgeben (Geld)
spill [spɪl]	spilt [spɪlt]	spilt [spɪlt]	*verschütten*
	spilled [spɪld]	spilled [spɪld]	
spin [spɪn]	spun [spʌn]	spun [spʌn]	*spinnen (Wolle)*
	span [spæn]		
spit [spɪt]	spat [spæt]	spat [spæt]	*spucken*
split [splɪt]	split [splɪt]	split [splɪt]	*spalten, (auf)schlitzen*
spoil [spɔɪl]	spoilt [spɔɪlt]	spoilt [spɔɪlt]	*verderben*
	spoiled [spɔɪld]	spoiled [spɔɪld]	
spread [spred]	spread [spred]	spread [spred]	*verbreiten, (sich) ausbreiten*
spring [sprɪŋ]	sprang [spræŋ]	sprung [sprʌŋ]	*springen*
stand [stænd]	stood [stʊd]	stood [stʊd]	*stehen*
steal [stiːl]	stole [stəʊl]	stolen ['stəʊlen]	*stehlen*
stick [stɪk]	stuck [stʌk]	stuck [stʌk]	*(an)stecken; (an)kleben*
sting [stɪŋ]	stung [stʌŋ]	stung [stʌŋ]	*stechen*

stink [stɪŋk]	stank [stæŋk] stunk [stʌŋk]	stunk [stʌŋk]	*stinken*
strike [straɪk]	struck [strʌk]	struck [strʌk]	*schlagen; stoßen; streiken*
strive [straɪv]	strove [strəʊv]	striven ['strɪvn]	*(an)streben*
swear [sweə]	swore [swɔː]	sworn [swɔːn]	*schwören; fluchen*
sweat [swet]	sweat [swet] sweated ['swetɪd]	sweat [swet] sweated ['swetɪd]	*schwitzen*
sweep [swiːp]	swept [swept]	swept [swept]	*fegen, kehren*
swell [swel]	swelled [sweld]	swollen ['swəʊlən] swelled [sweld]	*(an)schwellen*
swim [swɪm]	swam [swæm]	swum [swʌm]	*schwimmen*
swing [swɪŋ]	swung [swʌŋ]	swung [swʌŋ]	*schwingen; schwenken*
take [teɪk]	took [tʊk]	taken ['teɪkən]	*nehmen; (hin)bringen*
teach [tiːtʃ]	taught [tɔːt]	taught [tɔːt]	*lehren*
tear [teə]	tore [tɔː]	torn [tɔːn]	*zerreißen*
tell [tel]	told [təʊld]	told [təʊld]	*erzählen, (es) sagen*
think [θɪŋk]	thought [θɔːt]	thought [θɔːt]	*denken, glauben*
throw [θrəʊ]	threw [θruː]	thrown [θrəʊn]	*werfen*
tread [tred]	trod [trɒd]	trodden ['trɒdn] trod [trɒd]	*treten*
understand [ˌʌndə'stænd]	understood [ˌʌndə'stʊd]	understood [ˌʌndə'stʊd]	*verstehen*
wake [weɪk]	woke [wəʊk] waked [weɪkt]	woken ['wəʊkən] waked [weɪkt]	*(auf)wecken, -wachen*
wear [weə]	wore [wɔː]	worn [wɔːn]	*tragen (Kleidung); abnutzen*
weave [wiːv]	wove [wəʊv]	woven ['wəʊvən]	*weben*
weep [wiːp]	wept [wept]	wept [wept]	*weinen*
win [wɪn]	won [wʌn]	won [wʌn]	*gewinnen*
wind [waɪnd]	wound [waʊnd]	wound [waʊnd]	*winden; aufziehen (Uhr)*
write [raɪt]	wrote [rəʊt]	written ['rɪtn]	*schreiben*

Bildquellennachweis

Hewett Street Studios (Mike Mosedale), London: S. 7, 10, 27, 41, 44, 47, 57, 60, 82, 87, 89, 103
Hill and Mallet, Oxford University Press, Oxford: S. 13, 19, 63, 66, 71, 77, 91, 95, 100, 105, 108, 112
Punch, London: S. 16, 23, 25, 31, 36, 52